משנה הבריות

Who Makes People Different

Jewish Perspectives on People with Disabilities

RABBI CARL ASTOR

First edition edited by Rabbi Stephen Garfinkel

Revised edition edited by Karen L. Stein

UNITED SYNAGOGUE OF CONSERVATIVE JUDAISM
DEPARTMENT OF YOUTH ACTIVITIES

Jules A. Gutin, Director
Karen L. Stein, Assistant Director
Ezra Androphy, Activities Director
Ilana Clay, Program Coordinator
Sheridan Gayer, Education Coordinator
Jeremy Luski, Manager of Meetings and Special Events
Itzik Yanai, Central Shaliach
Yitzchak Jacobsen, Director, Israel Office
David Keren, Director, Israel Programs
Yossi Garr, Director, NATIV

INTERNATIONAL YOUTH COMMISSION
Robert Sunshine, Chair

UNITED SYNAGOGUE OF CONSERVATIVE JUDAISM
Dr. Ray Goldstein, International President
Rabbi Jerome M. Epstein, Executive Vice President
Dr. Marilyn Lishnoff Wind, Vice President of Youth and Education

A publication of the International Youth Commission
United Synagogue of Conservative Judaism
155 Fifth Avenue, New York, NY 10010
www.usy.org

Library of Congress Catalog Card Number: 84-52721
Revised Edition, Second Printing, 2005

Printed and bound in the United States of America by Howard Press.
Cover and book design by Karen L. Stein. Cover Artwork by Comstock Images.

Production, layout and design by Karen L. Stein, Project Editor

PREFACE TO REVISED EDITION

It was with some degree of surprise and a great deal of trepidation that I reacted to being asked to work on revising and updating a book that I had worked on over twenty years ago. What had changed during this period and what had not changed? Would any of the issues that we dealt with then be irrelevant or inconsequential twenty years later? Even the issue of terminology was a daunting one.

Fortunately, Karen Stein put together a competent and sensitive group of readers to help with the process. They were all constructive and gentle in their criticism, although I am sure that many aspects of the book were grating to them as language, ideas, and perceptions have changed so much in the course of time. So we looked for what in the book had more timeless meaning, what could be changed to remain relevant, and what new issues had arisen that needed to be addressed. We preserved what we could, changed what needed changing, and added new material.

Revisiting the subject of Judaism and disabilities reminded me of the sensitivity of this subject and the necessity to look at the sources with a critical eye; to learn from them and about them, and most importantly, to confront them with honesty and with careful attention.

It also inspired me to do more in my own synagogue with the problem of accessibility for those with handicaps. It is my hope that many of the people who read, teach and learn from this book will be inspired to become more active in the challenge of including everyone. I hope that it will cause us to reexamine our attitudes and prejudices, be they conscious or unconscious.

I want to thank all those who have participated in this effort, particularly the work of Karen in seeing the project through, and acknowledge that my involvement was more in the way of advising and reviewing the material. The real work was done by others, and without them this project would not have been accomplished.

Carl Astor
November, 2005

EDITOR'S PREFACE TO FIRST EDITION—Dr. Stephen Garfinkel

This volume has provoked controversy on a number of issues. The very title of the book, "...Who Makes People Different," has been viewed by some to be a negative assessment of those with disabilities. However, the wording, taken from the blessing recited upon seeing someone with a disability, is neutral. Being different is inherently neither good nor bad. Secondly, some of the terminology used in the source book—and, it must be stated, in the entire field of dealing with the disabled—is debated. Is it proper to speak of "the disabled" or must one refer to "those with disabilities"? Is it offensive to speak o someone's "handicap" or does one have a "disability"? These issues are dealt with in the sourcebook, but the debate continues. Finally, the very nature of the topic, considering Jewish attitudes towards those with disabilities, is a complicated matter. If our modern sensitivities sometimes differ from the attitudes or definitions assumed by early Jewish literature such as the Talmud, how do we react to it, and how can we apply the principles of our tradition to our current views and actions?

We are fortunate to have an author, Carl Astor, who was willing to confront these issues honestly and directly. Rabbi Astor has provided a wealth of material from a wide spectrum of sources. We must remember, therefore, that no one chapter of this volume stands on its own, but that together they contribute to our overall understanding of the topic. The thought and research Rabbi Astor has devoted to this project will provide us with an appreciation of the Jewish tradition as it has developed and continues to develop.

The manuscript draft has benefited from the suggestions of the following individuals, for whose expertise and guidance I am grateful:

Dr. Aryeh Davidson
Malka Edelman
Jane Epstein
Rabbi Paul Freedman
Judy Goldberg
Herb Greenberg
Rabbi Dan Grossman
Jules Gutin
Rabbi Benjamin Z. Kreitman
Chava Willig Levy
Rabbi Michael Levy
Richard Moline
Dr. Eduardo Rauch, z"l
Dr. David Soloff

I would also like to thank the following individuals for the assistance they offered: Joel Dickstein, Jonathan D. Draluck, Jerry Miller, Rev. Harold Wilke.

In addition, thanks go to Judith Sucher for typing the original manuscript and to Hellen Cutler for her help. I am grateful to Harry Silverman and Janet Asteroff who provided much technical assistance in this project, and Rabbi Akiva Lubow, who researched the Rabbinical Assembly Archives. Finally, my family, Robin, Arielle, and Talia, cannot be thanked sufficiently for all they have endured, yet another year.

In using this volume, let us remember that in many ways every person – each of us—is different.
S.G.

EDITOR'S PREFACE TO SECOND EDITION—Karen L. Stein

The publication of this revised edition marks the 20th anniversary of the initial publication, *M'Shaneh Habriyot*: Who Makes People Different. In the past 20 years, this book became one of the most popular sourcebooks published by the Department of Youth Activities. It has been used as the educational basis for countless conventions and *kinnusim*, encampments, and Hebrew High School courses. Additionally, it has served as a primary resource on the topic of the Jewish perspective on people with disabilities and has been cross-referenced in many other publications.

While *M'Shaneh Habriyot*: Who Makes People Different has remained as popular as ever in recent years, it became clearly apparent that this sourcebook had to be updated. In the past two decades, resources and advocacy for people with disabilities have evolved greatly and new doors have opened. Although the rabbinic texts have not changed, our understanding and translations of those texts had to. The scope of the topic is infinite, however, we choose to limit our exploration to a few types of disability that would serve as examples. Special attention was paid to terminology, using the most up-to-date terms and classifications. Words like "mute," "lame" and "retarded" were virtually eliminated and replaced with words that reflect dignity for a person with a disability.

This revised edition retains the format and general style of the original volume. Fortunately, Rabbi Astor agreed enthusiastically to help us update the book and began our process by guiding our path. We are privileged that many of the original readers were able to help us transform the text based upon what they have learned since 1984. Their insightful comments were invaluable towards producing a sourcebook which would be sensitive, current, and relevant:

Jane Epstein	Shelley Kaplan	Dr. Ora Horn Prouser
Rabbi Jerome M. Epstein	Judy Goldberg	Danny Siegel
Jonathan S. Greenberg	Jules Gutin	David Srebnick
		Gila Hadani Ward

Additionally, I am thankful to Roger Dela Cruz for typing the book into a 21st century format. I am particularly grateful to Jules Gutin for his review of the text and to Judy Goldberg. Judy truly became my *hevruta* (study partner) for this project and worked tirelessly to make sure that our definitions were correct and our approach to the topic was appropriate. Thank you for all of the articles, feedback and research.

I would also like to acknowledge new contributions for this edition from:

- Rabbi Bradley Shavit Artson, Dean, Ziegler School of Rabbinic Studies, Univ. of Judaism
- Jacob Artson, Author: "You Can Fly: Letting A Boy With Autism Speak for Himself"
- Rabbi Mitchell Cohen, Director, National Ramah Commission
- Rabbi Eliott Dorff, PhD, Rector, Sol & Anne Dorff Distinguished Service Professor in Philosophy, Co-Chair, Bioethics Dept., University of Judaism
- Judith E Goldberg, Director, Initiative for Women with Disabilities, Elly & Steve Hammerman Health & Wellness Cent, NYU--Hospital for Joint Diseases, NY
- Becca Hornstein, Executive Director, Council For Jews With Special Needs
- Shelley Kaplan, Chair, USCJ Commission on Accessibility
- Zivah Nativ, National Director Bar/Bat Mitzvah for the Special Child, Masorti Movement, Israel
- Sara Simon Rubinow, Chair, USCJ Committee on Jewish Special Education
- Danny Siegel, Ziv Tzedakah Foundation
- Ginny Thornburgh, National Organization on Disability

TABLE OF CONTENTS

Introduction—The Blessing

הרואה את ... המשנין בצורת פניהן או באבריהם מברך,
ברוך אתה ה' אלהינו מלך העולם משנה את הבריות.
הרואה סומא או קטע ומכה שחין ובוהקנין וכיוצא בהן מברך,
ברוך אתה ה' אלהינו מלך העולם דין האמת.
ואם נולדו כן ממעי אימן מברך, משנה את הבריות.

One who sees . . . people with disfigured faces or limbs, recites the blessing, **"Blessed are You, Lord our God, King of the universe, who makes people different."** One who sees a person who is blind or lame, or who is covered with sores and white pustules (or similar ailment), recites the blessing, **"Blessed are You, Lord our God, King of the universe, who is a righteous judge."** But if they were born that way (with the disability), one says, ". . .. who makes people different."

(Mishneh Torah, Hilchot B'rachot 10:12, based on B'rachot 58b)

At first these blessings may seem strange to us. Why should we single out someone who has a disfigurement, someone who is disabled, or people who look different from us for special attention? What is the meaning of these blessings? What is their function?

EXERCISE

Write out 4-5 other blessings you can think of, when they are recited, and why?

_____

_____

_____

_____

_____

_____

Why do you think we ever recite blessings?

For a Jew, reciting a blessing becomes a way of understanding the world. The blessing helps interpret the experience. Thus, for example, by reciting *hamotzi* when we eat bread, we interpret the availability of the food as an example of God's power and God's kindness to us. When we see a rainbow we say, "Blessed are You, Lord our God, King of the universe, who remembers the covenant, who is faithful to God's covenant and good to God's word". The blessing interprets the experience as an act of good faith, reminiscent of the original covenant made with Noah, that God would never again destroy the earth.

For Further Thought...

1. Does the fact that we say any *bracha* at all pose a problem? Why do you think we say *brachot* over a disability? Why are there two *brachot* and not only one? Do you see any problem with this? If so, what?

2. What do you feel like when you see someone of a different appearance?

3. Does a person's appearance affect the way we treat him?

4. Why do we single out people who seem different for special attention?

5. What is the meaning of the blessings? Why are there two different blessings?

6. The second blessing is used when we hear bad news, especially news of a death. Why do we say it here when we see someone who has a disability?

7. The *bracha* is recited as an expression of pain. Why?

The reason we say <u>this</u> blessing is that seeing an individual who is so dramatically different from us gives us the opportunity to appreciate all differences among people. It is the wonder that elicits the blessing, and the blessing that interprets the wonder.

The *Mishnah* brings a beautiful analogy, comparing God with one who stamps coins:

> (An individual man was created) to show the greatness of God. While a person stamps many coins from a single die, and they are all alike, the King of kings has stamped every person with the die of Adam, yet not one of them is like his fellow.
>
> *(Sanhedrin 4:5)*

"THE RIGHTEOUS JUDGE"

The second blessing, "…. Who is a righteous judge," is quite different from the first. This is the *b'rachah* which is to be said when we hear bad news, especially news of a death. Yet we say it here upon seeing someone who is blind, unable to walk properly, or suffering from an awful disease. Why?

A hint may be found in the *Shulchan Aruch*, a sixteenth century code of Jewish law. Its author, Joseph Karo, explains the law by adding, "…. And some say (this *brachah* should be said) only for a person one cares about."[i]

In other words, if the person who has a disability is someone whom you despise, or for whom you feel no closeness, then you should not say the blessing.

> ➤ **Do you agree that you should only say the *bracha* for someone you like?**

> ➤ **Why does the *Shulchan Aruch* say that you shouldn't say the *bracha* if you don't feel close to the person?**

> ➤ **What do you think the *Shulchan Aruch* is trying to teach us?**

Thus, the *bracha* is recited as an expression of our pain. We say "righteous judge" because we feel badly when we see someone who appears to be suffering. Yes, we may accept God's judgment, that in God's infinite wisdom God has allowed this to happen, but we grieve nevertheless. If one encounters a person whose disabling condition is congenital (i.e., something the person has from birth), the *bracha* changes to "who makes people different."

> ➤ **Why do we say a different *bracha* if the person was born with a disability as opposed to if they were hurt later in life causing the disability?**

This happens because the affliction did not result from an accident or a disease but was, rather, a natural condition of birth. So, for instance, some people have 20/20 vision, some wear glasses and some are blind. Put simply, such conditions are part of the natural variety of life.

> ➤ **Do you agree that there should be two blessings?**

"Righteous judge" refers to our acceptance of God's will and our inability to understand it. Yet, we still feel badly when we see someone suffering.

> **"First become a blessing to yourself that you may be a blessing to others."**
>
> **--Rabbi Samson Raphael Hirsch**

WHO MAKES PEOPLE UNIQUE

The blessing "…. Who makes people different" may be a way of highlighting the uniqueness of each individual. Just because people are different does not mean that they are inferior. The Midrash makes this point, again bringing the story of creation to teach the uniqueness and ultimate value of each human being.

> Man was created as a single individual to teach you that anyone who destroys a single life is as though he destroyed an entire world, and anyone who preserves a single life is as though he preserved an entire world. (The creation of an individual being was done) also for the sake of peace among mankind, that no person should say to another, "My father is greater than your father."
>
> *(Sanhedrin 4:5)*

Just because a person has a disability does not mean that he or she necessarily has less to contribute or is in any meaningful way less of a human being that one who is "normal". The degree to which a person may be limited, of course, depends on the type and severity of disability and the individual.

Ralph Barton Perry writes the following in his introduction to Helen Keller's *The Story of My Life:*

> The important fact is that when she lost her sight and hearing she did not lose her mind. She can think, compare, remember, anticipate, associate, imagine, speculate, and feel. Her world contains the same dimensions as other peoples' worlds and admits her to the same universe of discourse and to full participation in the life about her. Endowed by nature with a high degree of general activity, with a zestful, playful and buoyant temperament, and with a strong impulse to express and communicate, she has gone out to meet life and learn the lessons it teaches.[ii]

Perry then goes on to make one of the classic and most profound statements which applies to all of us: "It is true that Helen Keller is 'handicapped'—as indeed, who is not? But what distinguishes her is not her handicap but the extent to which she has overcome it, and even profited by it."

> **Helen Keller**, at the age of 19 months, suddenly lost her hearing and vision, and, against overwhelming odds and with a great deal of persistence, grew into a highly intelligent and sensitive woman who wrote, spoke, and labored incessantly for the betterment of others.

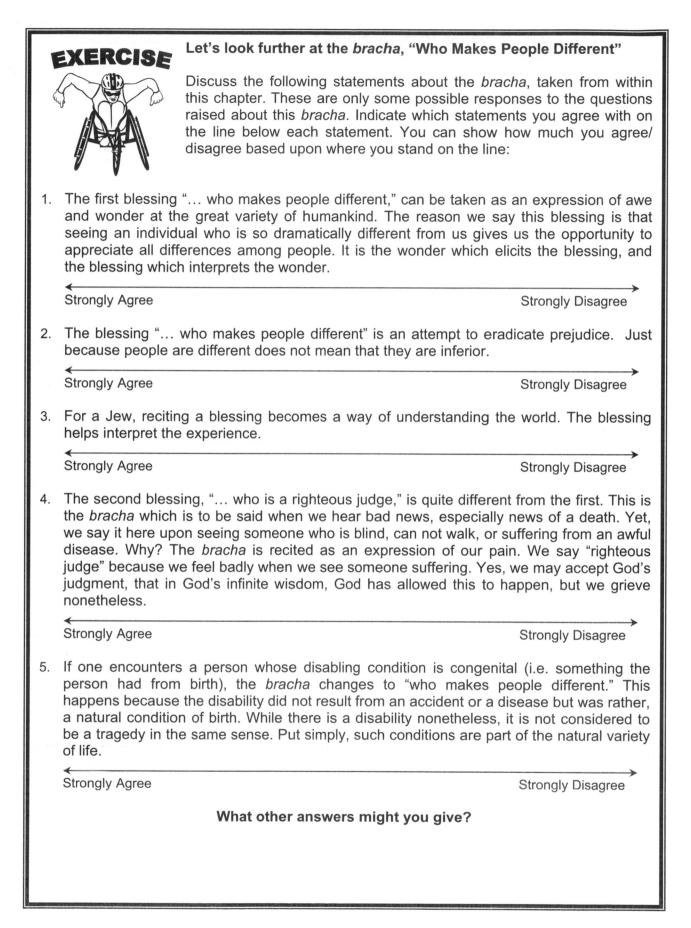

EXERCISE

Let's look further at the *bracha*, "Who Makes People Different"

Discuss the following statements about the *bracha*, taken from within this chapter. These are only some possible responses to the questions raised about this *bracha*. Indicate which statements you agree with on the line below each statement. You can show how much you agree/disagree based upon where you stand on the line:

1. The first blessing "… who makes people different," can be taken as an expression of awe and wonder at the great variety of humankind. The reason we say this blessing is that seeing an individual who is so dramatically different from us gives us the opportunity to appreciate all differences among people. It is the wonder which elicits the blessing, and the blessing which interprets the wonder.

   ←——————————————————————————————→
   Strongly Agree   Strongly Disagree

2. The blessing "… who makes people different" is an attempt to eradicate prejudice. Just because people are different does not mean that they are inferior.

   ←——————————————————————————————→
   Strongly Agree   Strongly Disagree

3. For a Jew, reciting a blessing becomes a way of understanding the world. The blessing helps interpret the experience.

   ←——————————————————————————————→
   Strongly Agree   Strongly Disagree

4. The second blessing, "… who is a righteous judge," is quite different from the first. This is the *bracha* which is to be said when we hear bad news, especially news of a death. Yet, we say it here upon seeing someone who is blind, can not walk, or suffering from an awful disease. Why? The *bracha* is recited as an expression of our pain. We say "righteous judge" because we feel badly when we see someone suffering. Yes, we may accept God's judgment, that in God's infinite wisdom, God has allowed this to happen, but we grieve nonetheless.

   ←——————————————————————————————→
   Strongly Agree   Strongly Disagree

5. If one encounters a person whose disabling condition is congenital (i.e. something the person had from birth), the *bracha* changes to "who makes people different." This happens because the disability did not result from an accident or a disease but was rather, a natural condition of birth. While there is a disability nonetheless, it is not considered to be a tragedy in the same sense. Put simply, such conditions are part of the natural variety of life.

   ←——————————————————————————————→
   Strongly Agree   Strongly Disagree

What other answers might you give?

How Does Jewish Tradition View Disability?

As we examine Jewish attitudes towards people with disabilities, it is important to understand that there is not a monolithic view on this matter.

First, there is the question of treatment of people with disabilities. Here we will discover that those with disabilities were placed in a category similar to any people who are weak and vulnerable: the poor, the orphan, the widow, the stranger. They must be protected and helped so that they can live good lives and not suffer from abject poverty and neglect. Just as we were once weak strangers in the land of Egypt, so they are in a similar position in our society.

Second, there is the purely legal aspect relating to people with disabilities. Here the discussions appear to be much more objective and of a practical nature. What ritual requirements can be fulfilled by the people with disabilities and which cannot? What are the limits of responsibility to and of people with disabilities? The answers to such questions do not appear to be decided only on the basis of attitudes but also according to the legal necessities of each case.

Third, there is the midrashic view to which we have already been introduced in this section. This approach is often linked to the intrinsic value of each individual.

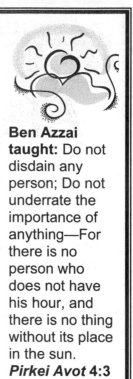

Ben Azzai taught: Do not disdain any person; Do not underrate the importance of anything—For there is no person who does not have his hour, and there is no thing without its place in the sun.
Pirkei Avot 4:3

Fourth, we will examine the theological implications of having a disability. Often the way an individual feels about himself or herself is dependent upon one's view of how he or she appears in the eyes of God. Does Jewish theology have anything to say about this matter?

Finally, we must look at the services for people with disabilities provided by the Jewish community. Concern or lack of concern is accurately measured in concrete actions as well as in words.

For Further Thought...

> ➤ **What is your attitude towards individuals with disabilities?**

> ➤ **Is there a difference between "caring" and "patronizing"?**

> ➤ **Are your views toward individuals with disabilities reflected in your actions?**

EXERCISE The following questions should be considered before you begin reading of this volume. After you have completed your study of the topic, consider them once again. Answer as honestly and frankly as possible.

1. Do you feel that Judaism has generally had a liberal, open-minded view toward those with disabilities?

2. Are there any ritual actions from which a person with a disability should be excluded?

3. What does the following biblical phrase mean to you: Do not put a stumbling block in front of the blind; do not curse the deaf?

4. Can a disability ever be a blessing? If so, how?

5. Did you ever have friend who has a disability? If so, did you ever ask him or her how it feels to have a disability? If you didn't have a friend who has a disability, were there any particular reasons?

6. Do you feel that Jewish institutions are generally accessible to people with disabilities? What about your synagogue?

7. Do you think that people who have an intellectual impairment should get married or have children?

8. Should someone who is deaf have a Bar/ Bat mitzvah? What about someone who is blind? What about someone who has an intellectual impairment?

9. Why do you think some people are born with disabilities and others are not? Does this raise any questions for you about God?

10. Are there any recent developments which might, in your opinion, change Jewish views toward people with disabilities?

Chapter One-- Defining Terms

There is an important distinction to be made between the terms "handicapped" and "disabled." A handicap is a societal burden, not necessarily related to a person's physical or mental condition. There are many handicapped people who are in no way "disabled." A disability on the other hand is a physical or mental condition. It is a handicap in the sense that it places an additional burden upon the individual, but it in no way diminishes that individual's potential— society does that.

In the past, it was extremely difficult, if not impossible, for people who were disabled to find employment. The word "handicap" originated because with no financial income many had to resort to begging. It was common when begging to hold out a cap in hand so people could drop in coins -- they had their cap handy... or had a "handy cap." *Eventually, this term applied to all people with disabilities.* It is inappropriate to use this prejudicial term.

As you refer to people who have disabilities, it is important to mention the person first and the disability second. These statements are okay:
> We are going to learn about people with disabilities.
> A person who is blind...
> A person who uses a wheelchair…

These statements are NOT okay because the emphasis is on the disability:
> We are going to learn about disabled people.
> A blind person...
> A wheelchair-bound person...

EXERCISE   **List as many types or categories of disabilities you can think of. Do you know anyone personally who has that kind of disability?**

TERMINOLOGY

Under the American with Disabilities Act[iii], an individual with a disability is a person who:

- has a physical or mental impairment that substantially limits one or more major life activities;
- has a record of such an impairment; or
- is regarded as having such an impairment.

A **physical impairment** is defined by the ADA as "Any physiological disorder or condition, cosmetic disfigurement, or anatomical loss affecting one or more of the following body systems: neurological, musculoskeletal, special sense organs, respiratory (including speech organs), cardiovascular, reproductive, digestive, genitourinary, hemic and lymphatic, skin, and endocrine."

A **mental impairment** is defined by the ADA as "[a]ny mental or psychological disorder, such as mental retardation, organic brain syndrome, emotional or mental illness, and specific learning disabilities."

An impairment under the ADA is a physiological or mental disorder; simple physical characteristics, therefore, such as eye or hair color, left-handedness, or height or weight within a normal range, are not impairments. A physical condition that is not the result of a physiological disorder, such as pregnancy, or a predisposition to a certain disease would not be an impairment. Similarly, personality traits such as poor judgment, quick temper or irresponsible behavior, are not themselves impairments. Environmental, cultural, or economic disadvantages, such as lack of education or a prison record also are not impairments.

> Example: A person who cannot read due to dyslexia is an individual with a disability because of dyslexia, which is a learning disability, and is an impairment. But a person who cannot read because she dropped out of school is not an individual with a disability, because lack of education is not an impairment.

People with disabilities are just that, people. They have the same desire to participate in, and contribute to their communities as everyone else. They also have the same desire as everyone else to be treated with dignity and respect. People with disabilities are whole people. Having a disability is only one aspect of a person's life. There are many more parts to a person's life than simply having a disability. For example, someone may be an artist, father, employer, friend and also be a person with a disability.

The terminology used in classifying individuals with disabilities is often quite detailed and confusing. Listed below are general classifications covering the basic categories of people with disabilities:[iv]

> People who have **mental retardation** (or people who have a developmental disability or intellectual impairment), that is, with significantly below average intelligence, vary widely in the severity of the disability. Some are educable, i.e., they can be educated, socially adjusted to home and community, hold a job, and be self supporting or partially self supporting as adults. Some are trainable, i.e., they learn self-care skills, socially adjust to home or immediate neighborhood, and can do some tasks in the home or sheltered workshop. Others are totally dependent and require institutional care.

> Individuals with **sensory disabilities** have impairments in vision or hearing. Since here, too, there are varying degrees of disability, the manner in which the person with a disability learns will differ depending on a variety of factors. A person may be blind or

partially sighted). Others may be deaf or, with a milder form of disability, hard of hearing.

When referring to **learning disabilities**, use the terms "learning disabilities" and "children with special needs". Specific disabilities include "attention deficit disorder (ADD)", dyslexia, speech impairment, etc. Never use the term "normal" in contrast.

Persons who have **orthopedic disabilities** include those who have mobility impairments from various causes, some being from birth and others resulting from disease or accident.

People with **neurological impairments** are the most numerous in the special needs categories. There are many degrees of disabilities due to damage of the nervous system, and intelligence is affected in about half of these cases. A few neurological disorders have been found to be Jewish genetic diseases.

Communication disorders include a wide variety of speech defects. Learning disabilities, difficulties in understanding or using spoken or written language, are also forms of communication or perceptual disorders. Learning disabled people, however, may have adequate motor ability, average to high intelligence, and adequate emotional adjustment.

Behavior disorders include a range of emotional maladjustments (like anxiety, neuroticism, extreme inner tensions, or psychotic behavior) or social maladjustments (in which the individual shows generally antisocial behavior).

Persons who have **multiple-disabilities** have more than one of the impairments listed above. For instance, one might have cerebral palsy and developmental disabilities, or be deaf and blind, or have severe physical disabilities and learning disabilities.

As you follow the rest of this book, you can see how Judaism has viewed people with disabilities historically and how its changing attitudes have paralleled or differed from those of the rest of Western civilization.

Having a Disability, Doesn't Mean a Person is Disabled[v]
Having a physical difference doesn't automatically make a person disabled. Many factors come into play: attitudes, the percentage of the population with the same physical difference, and environmental accommodations are just a few.

For example, most people who wear glasses don't think of themselves as being visually disabled. Yet, eyeglasses and contact lenses are corrections for a vision disability. With this special accommodation, people are able to work, play, and live in their communities. In our society, wearing eyeglasses or contacts has become so acceptable that we don't think of it as an accommodation for a physical limitation.

Everyone Uses Technology To Do What Their Bodies Cannot
A thousand years ago, we used horses and oxen to compensate for the inability of our legs to travel great distances in a safe and timely manner. Hundreds of years later, we designed devices that moved us faster, further, and more comfortably. Today, we matter-of-factly use technology to change our environment to accomplish what our bodies cannot. In fact, our feet cannot carry us in the same amount of time, or with the same amount of comfort as planes,

cars, and even shoes can. We are so used to the idea of controlling the world around us that we forget just how dependent we are on the devices we've created. For example:

1. Transportation
- Planes. We are able to travel from coast to coast in about five hours. Several centuries ago, the same trip would have taken a lifetime by foot.
- Cars. We can jump on a bus or in a car and go 60 miles in just one hour.
- Shoes. We have even built foot coverings (shoes) which not only protect our feet, but enable us to jump higher and run faster.

2. Communication
- Speech. Without help our voices will carry only a few yards. With a phone we can talk to someone hundreds or thousands of miles away.
- Hearing. Our ears have a limited listening range. Yet with a phone or radio we listen to information and entertainment from nearly everywhere in the world.
- Sight. With television we can see well beyond the limits of our eyes. We can see real-time events and pictures from all over the world. Eyeglasses and contact lenses help us to see when our vision isn't 20/20.

Word Power
Words are very powerful. They are like the paint an artist uses to express their impressions of the world around them. We use words in the same way. With words, we paint the limits and possibilities of our reality. Perhaps the language we use is the most telling example of how we perceive the value of people with disabilities in our society.

Words are very powerful. They reinforce our ideas of who we are and who and what we expect we can be. Avoid using words which suggest helplessness or infirmity, such as: crippled, victim, handicapped, disabled or invalid. (This last word actually comes from the phrase "in-valid.") Since having a disability is a part of the lives of people with disabilities, generally speaking, it is not a good idea to totally drop any reference to the disability. However, it is healthy to try to put the disability into the context of the whole person.

There are always exceptions to every rule. Generally speaking, when you are describing a person with a disability, we should use words that emphasize the personhood, wholeness, and abilities of the person. Such as: "person with cerebral palsy", "person with a vision disability", "person with a hearing disability." However, when a term has gained intrinsic strength among a large group of persons with a specific disability, the personhood rule may be suspended in favor of political or cultural preferences. For example: "The Deaf" -- This term is considered culturally appropriate and is preferred over the terms "persons who are deaf" or "persons with hearing disabilities" by international organizations of people who are deaf.

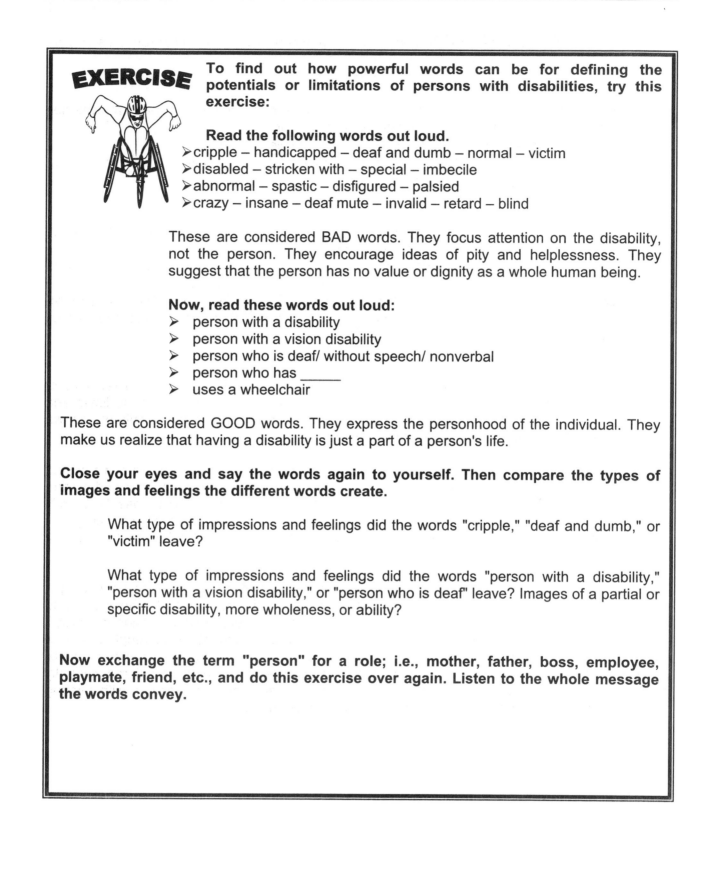

EXERCISE

To find out how powerful words can be for defining the potentials or limitations of persons with disabilities, try this exercise:

Read the following words out loud.
➢ cripple – handicapped – deaf and dumb – normal – victim
➢ disabled – stricken with – special – imbecile
➢ abnormal – spastic – disfigured – palsied
➢ crazy – insane – deaf mute – invalid – retard – blind

These are considered BAD words. They focus attention on the disability, not the person. They encourage ideas of pity and helplessness. They suggest that the person has no value or dignity as a whole human being.

Now, read these words out loud:
➢ person with a disability
➢ person with a vision disability
➢ person who is deaf/ without speech/ nonverbal
➢ person who has _____
➢ uses a wheelchair

These are considered GOOD words. They express the personhood of the individual. They make us realize that having a disability is just a part of a person's life.

Close your eyes and say the words again to yourself. Then compare the types of images and feelings the different words create.

What type of impressions and feelings did the words "cripple," "deaf and dumb," or "victim" leave?

What type of impressions and feelings did the words "person with a disability," "person with a vision disability," or "person who is deaf" leave? Images of a partial or specific disability, more wholeness, or ability?

Now exchange the term "person" for a role; i.e., mother, father, boss, employee, playmate, friend, etc., and do this exercise over again. Listen to the whole message the words convey.

WORDS WITH DIGNITY-- Encouraging Equality for Everyone

Words With Dignity	Avoid These Words
person with a disability	cripple/handicapped/handicap/invalid (Literally, invalid means "not valid." Don't use it.)
person who has/person who experienced/person with (e.g., person who has cerebral palsy)	victim/afflicted by/afflicted with (e.g., victim of cerebral palsy)
uses a wheelchair	restricted, confined to a wheelchair/wheelchair bound (The chair enables mobility. Without the chair, the person is confined to bed.)
non-disabled	normal (Referring to non-disabled persons as "normal" insinuates that people with disabilities are abnormal.)
deaf/without speech/nonverbal	deaf mute/deaf and dumb
disabled since birth/born with a disability	birth defect
person with mental illness	crazy/insane
seizures	fits
developmental disability	slow

Chapter Two—Biblical Sources

IN ANCIENT TIMES...

In order to understand current Jewish attitudes toward people with disabilities, it will be of benefit to look at those views as they have developed through history. We begin, therefore, with ancient times and, most specifically, with the biblical period.

As with many ideas, laws and theology, biblical attitudes towards people with disabilities can best be understood in their historic and cultural setting. It is important, therefore, to see the *Tanakh* (Hebrew Bible) against the background of its times. In most ancient civilizations disabilities were seen as signs of disgrace, usually taken as a sign of displeasure from the gods.

The *Tanakh's* attitude towards people with disabilities clearly reflects their civilization. In ancient times people who were blind or could not use their legs were quite numerous and were often kept outside of the cities. They might remain there as paupers, begging and presenting a danger to those who would enter. This even became a subject for taunting the enemy, as the Jebusites said to David when he came to conquer Jerusalem from them:

וַיֵּ֨לֶךְ הַמֶּ֤לֶךְ וַאֲנָשָׁיו֙ יְר֣וּשָׁלִַ֔ם אֶל־הַיְבֻסִ֖י יוֹשֵׁ֣ב הָאָ֑רֶץ וַיֹּ֤אמֶר לְדָוִד֙
לֵאמֹר֙ לֹא־תָב֣וֹא הֵ֔נָּה כִּ֣י אִם־הֱסִֽירְךָ֗ הַעִוְרִ֤ים וְהַפִּסְחִים֙ לֵאמֹ֔ר לֹא־יָב֥וֹא
דָוִ֖ד הֵֽנָּה׃ וַיִּלְכֹּ֣ד דָּוִ֔ד אֵ֖ת מְצֻדַ֣ת צִיּ֑וֹן הִ֖יא עִ֥יר דָּוִֽד׃ וַיֹּ֨אמֶר דָּוִ֜ד בַּיּ֣וֹם
הַה֗וּא כָּל־מַכֵּ֤ה יְבֻסִי֙ וְיִגַּ֣ע בַּצִּנּ֔וֹר וְאֶת־הַפִּסְחִ֥ים וְאֶת־הַֽעִוְרִ֖ים שְׂנֻאֵ֣י
[שְׂנֻאֵ֣י] נֶ֣פֶשׁ דָּוִ֑ד עַל־כֵּן֙ יֹֽאמְר֔וּ עִוֵּ֣ר וּפִסֵּ֔חַ לֹ֥א יָב֖וֹא אֶל־הַבָּֽיִת׃

Unless you can remove the blind and one who can not walk, you shall not come here" (thinking: David is unable to come here). Nevertheless, David captured the stronghold of Zion, which is now the City of David. On that occasion David said, "Those who attack the Jebusites, shall reach the water channel and (strike down) the lame and the blind, who are hateful to David." That is why they say, "No one who is blind or lame may enter the House."

(II Samuel 5:6-8)

➤ **Is this saying to be construed as degrading to a person who is blind or can not walk? Or, was it simply a reaction to the insult directed at David?**

➤ **Was David's reaction reasonable, or could he have reacted differently?**

➤ **What attitude, if an, does this source reflect toward people with disabilities?**

The Biblical Perspective

The view of the *Tanakh* towards people with disabilities differs dramatically from that of many other primitive cultures. Generally God is not pictured as punishing people by afflicting them with physical infirmities or disabilities. Even Miriam, who is stricken with some type of skin disease as a result of her disparaging remarks about her brother Moses, suffers only a temporary ailment, during which she is kept out of the camp:

וַיֹּאמֶר יְהוָה אֶל־מֹשֶׁה וְאָבִיהָ יָרֹק יָרַק בְּפָנֶיהָ הֲלֹא
תִכָּלֵם שִׁבְעַת יָמִים תִּסָּגֵר שִׁבְעַת
יָמִים מִחוּץ לַמַּחֲנֶה וְאַחַר תֵּאָסֵף׃

But the Lord said to Moses, "If her father spat in her face, would she not bear her shame for seven days? Let her be shut out of camp seven days, and then let her be readmitted."

(*Bamidbar* 12:14)

➢ **What was Miriam's disability? What caused it?**

➢ **Was this punishment from God justified? Why did it take the form of a debilitating illness?**

➢ **What was the community's reaction? Why is she sent out from the camp?**

➢ **How does our attitude towards people with AIDS or other sexually-transmitted diseases compare with the biblical attitude towards leprosy?**

From this passage we learn that it was not the disease itself that was seen as shameful, but rather the cause of the disease—Miriam's slandering of Moses. In general, people with this ailment were kept outside of the camp not because of disgrace or shame, but to protect the rest of the community from the disease and its ritual impurity that they believed to be contagious.

EXERCISE

List at least three Biblical figures, their disabilities, and what impact it had on the character's life.

BIBLICAL FIGURE	DISABILITY	IMPACT ON CHARACTER

Biblical Heroes

The major figures of the *Tanakh* were far from physically perfect. Among other possible disabilities, Isaac was blind at least part of his life:

וַיְהִי כִּי־זָקֵן יִצְחָק וַתִּכְהֶיןָ עֵינָיו מֵרְאֹת וַיִּקְרָא אֶת־עֵשָׂו | בְּנוֹ הַגָּדֹל וַיֹּאמֶר אֵלָיו בְּנִי וַיֹּאמֶר אֵלָיו הִנֵּנִי׃

When Isaac was old and his eyes were too dim to see…

(*Bereshit* 27:1)

We know today that children born to older parents may have a higher risk of birth defects. Could this have been the case with Isaac? Could *Akaidat Yitzchak* (the Binding of Isaac) been an attempt by Abraham to get rid of a child with a defect?

וַתַּהַר וַתֵּלֶד שָׂרָה לְאַבְרָהָם בֵּן לִזְקֻנָיו לַמּוֹעֵד אֲשֶׁר־דִּבֶּר אֹתוֹ אֱלֹהִים׃

Sarah conceived and bore a son to Abraham in his old age, at the set time of which God had spoken.

(*Bereshit* 21:2)

Jacob, too, was certainly not the heroic type, socially or physically. Jacob had difficulty walking for much of his life, and ends up as blind as his father, Isaac. Jacob's brother Esau is the stronger, more "manly" son, yet, in the eyes of the *Tanakh*, it is Jacob who is superior and destined to carry on the Jewish line. Nor were the matriarchs pictured as being perfect or unblemished. Sarah, Rebekah and Rachel are all barren….(and) Leah, while not barren, has weak eyes.

➢ **What can we learn from the imperfections of the patriarchs and matriarchs?**

Even more astonishing is that perhaps the greatest biblical hero of them all, Moses, is described as having a limitation connected with his speech:

וַיַּעַן מֹשֶׁה וַיֹּאמֶר וְהֵן לֹא־יַאֲמִינוּ לִי וְלֹא יִשְׁמְעוּ בְּקֹלִי כִּי יֹאמְרוּ לֹא־נִרְאָה אֵלֶיךָ יְהֹוָה׃

But Moses spoke up and said, "What if they do not believe me and do not listen to me, but say: The Lord did not appear to you?"

(*Shemot* 4:1)

וַיֹּאמֶר מֹשֶׁה אֶל־יְהֹוָה בִּי אֲדֹנָי לֹא מַאֲמִינ אָנֹכִי גַּם מִתְּמוֹל גַּם מִשִּׁלְשֹׁם גַּם מֵאָז דַּבֶּרְךָ אֶל־עַבְדֶּךָ כִּי כְבַד־פֶּה וּכְבַד לָשׁוֹן אָנֹכִי׃

But Moses said to the Lord, "Please, O Lord, I have never been a man of words, either in times past or now that you have spoken to Your servant; I am slow of speech and slow of tongue."

(*Shemot* 4:10)

God's answer to Moses is most instructive:

וַיֹּאמֶר יְהוָה אֵלָיו מִי שָׂם פֶּה לָאָדָם אוֹ
מִי־יָשׂוּם אִלֵּם אוֹ חֵרֵשׁ אוֹ פִקֵּחַ אוֹ עִוֵּר הֲלֹא אָנֹכִי יְהוָה: וְעַתָּה לֵךְ
וְאָנֹכִי אֶהְיֶה עִם־פִּיךָ וְהוֹרֵיתִיךָ אֲשֶׁר תְּדַבֵּר:

> And the Lord said to him, "Who gives man speech? Who makes him unable to speak or deaf, seeing or blind? Is it not I, the Lord? Now go, and I will be with you as you speak and will instruct you what to say."

> (*Shemot* 4:11-12)

God tells Moses not to regard his disability as a barrier to his mission; indeed, it is just the opposite. There is a hidden purpose to the impairment and Moses must fulfill his destiny. The disability is no disgrace or shame: it is a challenge with a purpose. Moses is destined to rise up above his peers, above all of Egypt, and it will eventually be his speech limitation that may be one of the few factors which keep his people from mistaking him for God Himself.

For Further Thought…

1. **Why was Moses so hesitant to act as a spokesperson for God?**

2. **Why does God insist that Moses act as God's spokesperson despite his disability?**

3. **What does that tell us about God's attitude towards people with disabilities?**

4. **In this text, Moses cites his poor speaking ability as a reason for him not to be God's chosen emissary. Are there any impediments that keep you from speaking as a leader?**

5. **What message can we learn from God's choice of a person with a speech impediment as God's spokesperson?**

6. **The Hebrew text uses the term *k'vad*, literally, heavy mouth and heavy tongue, to describe Moses' manner of speaking. What issues or words weigh heavily upon our tongues, making I difficult for us to express them publicly?**

7. **How does knowing that Moses had an impairment compare to our secular concept of a spokesperson or a leader?**

Biblical Sensitivity to Needs and Feelings

Biblical law is an accurate barometer of the trends and attitudes of ancient society. The *Tanakh* regards all forms of disability as weaknesses which make one especially vulnerable. In society at large, there was a tendency to abuse the weak and defenseless, the poor, the widow, the orphan, and the stranger. The *Tanakh* champions their cause, repeatedly warning against such abuse, warning that the cry of those who have no voice will be heard by God who loves the weak.

For instance, words of wisdom in Proverbs, just before the section describing the ideal wife (*eshet hayil*), demand that one extend oneself on behalf of those who need help:

פְּתַח־פִּיךָ לְאִלֵּם אֶל־דִּין כָּל־בְּנֵי חֲלוֹף׃
פְּתַח־פִּיךָ שְׁפָט־צֶדֶק וְדִין עָנִי וְאֶבְיוֹן׃

> Speak up for those who can not speak, for the rights of all the unfortunate.
> Speak up, judge righteously, champion the poor and the needy.

(Proverbs 31:8)

That there is a specific law forbidding the abuse of the blind and the deaf may attest to the common tendency in biblical times to disregard people with disabilities:

לֹא־תְקַלֵּל חֵרֵשׁ וְלִפְנֵי עִוֵּר לֹא
תִתֵּן מִכְשֹׁל וְיָרֵאתָ מֵּאֱלֹהֶיךָ אֲנִי יְהֹוָה׃

> You shall not insult the deaf, or place a stumbling before the blind. You shall fear your God: I am the Lord.

(Vayikra 19:14)

> ➤ **How do you understand this verse? What is it trying to say?**

> ➤ **How could we apply Lev. 19:14 to the obligation of synagogues to be more accessible to those with disabilities?**

> **See Chapter Seven for suggestions for making synagogues more accessible to people with disabilities.**

This law can be understood on two levels. Of course there is the literal meaning of shielding those with disabilities from cruelty and insensitivity where they are most vulnerable. Taking advantage of a person's disability for sadistic, economic or any other reasons was strictly forbidden.

הוּא הָיָה אוֹמֵר, אִם אֵין אֲנִי לִי, מִי לִי.
וּכְשֶׁאֲנִי לְעַצְמִי, מָה אֲנִי. וְאִם לֹא עַכְשָׁיו, אֵימָתַי׃

> He (Hillel) used to say, If I am not for me, who am I? If I am not for myself, who will be for be? If not now, when?

(Pirke Avot 1:14)

> ➤ **Based upon the above text, how would Hillel approach the text about not putting a stumbling block before the blind?**

> ➤ **What is Hillel saying about the world around us?**

The Rabbis interpreted the law in a more figurative manner, as Rashi (a famous 11th century commentator on the *Tanakh* and Talmud) explains, "Before the blind in a certain matter." In other words, if one has a lacking, a "blind spot," in a certain area, we must not be insensitive to that weakness or take unfair advantage of it.

> ➤ **Can you give an example of this interpretation of the law? What might be considered a "blind spot"?**

To us (and probably the Biblical commentators), this verse seems to be stating the obvious. Of course it is wrong to place an obstacle in front of a person who is blind, but, as Dr. Morton Siegel explains:

> … In ancient traditions, those who were physically impaired were not uncommonly viewed as "cursed of God" and if "cursed of God," why not cursed of man? Do you pass legislation telling people not to do something unless they have been doing it? Obviously they have been doing it.

Biblical law created its own system in which the physically impaired and "the special" must not be subject to exploitation or to demeaning. It also outlines specific instances where we must go out of our way to protect others who may not be able to protect themselves:

כִּי תִבְנֶה בַּיִת חָדָשׁ וְעָשִׂיתָ

מַעֲקֶה לְגַגֶּךָ וְלֹא־תָשִׂים דָּמִים בְּבֵיתֶךָ כִּי־יִפֹּל הַנֹּפֵל מִמֶּנּוּ׃

When you build a new house, you shall make a parapet for your roof, so that you do not bring bloodguilt on your house if anyone should fall from it.

(*D'varim* 22:8)

> ➤ **Why does the text insist on having a protective fence?**

> ➤ **Shouldn't falling off be the responsibility of the person that went up on the roof in the first place?**

> ➤ **What is the torah saying here about the need to protect others?**

A Different View

Rabbi Elliot Dorff, at the University of Judaism offers us a kinder explanation for our tradition's treatment of disabilities[vi]:

> "I think it is fair to say from the very start that traditional Judaism's approach to disability is remarkably enlightened and compassionate, especially when compared to the treatment disabled people got in other cultures… Note that almost all of the biblical heroes were disabled in some way. Sarah, Rebekah, Rachel, and Hannah are all barren for some time in their lives, Isaac and Jacob suffer from blindness in their old age, Jacob was lame for much of his life, and even the greatest biblical hero, Moses, suffered from a speech impediment. Similarly, a number of Talmudic rabbis were disabled; for example, Nahum of Gimzo, Dosa ben Harkinas, Rav Joseph, and Rav Sheshet were all blind. The more "manly" biblical models – Esau, Gideon, Samson, and even David – are all

portrayed as flawed in character. In contrast, the heroes of Greek and Roman culture were all physically perfect -- even extraordinary…. The fact that so many of the biblical and rabbinic heroes were disabled in various ways speaks volumes about how our tradition from its very beginnings thought of this group of people: in contrast to the Greek, Roman, and American cultures, in Jewish sources people with disabilities were to be construed like everyone else, and they were often leaders.

"…For the Jewish tradition, we are all created in the image of God, and, as such, we have divine worth independent of whatever we do. That does not mean that we may do whatever we want; quite the contrary, God gives us 613 commandments, and the Rabbis add many more. Moreover, the fact that each person is created in the image of God does not mean that we have to like everyone or what everyone does. It does mean, though, that even when we judge a person harshly for his or her actions, we must still recognize the divine worth inherent in that person. …

"The Jewish tradition is remarkable not only in how it thought about people with disabilities, but in the actions it demanded with and for them. In Greek and Roman cultures, "imperfect" infants were put out to die, and disabled adults were left to fend for themselves and often mocked to boot. In Jewish culture, in contrast, killing an infant for any reason constitutes murder, and the Torah specifically prohibits cursing the deaf or putting a stumbling block before the blind.

"With this as a background, though, it is also important that we acknowledge that Jewish sources did put people with disabilities at some disadvantage. This especially affected the Temple and the biblical concept of the holy. Specifically, while disabled men born into the priestly class were not denied their part of the priestly portions, they were not allowed to serve in the Temple and were instead put to menial work such as cleaning the kindling wood from worms, for which a special area was set aside: "No one at all who has a defect shall be qualified [to offer a sacrifice], no man who is blind, or lame, or has a limb too short or too long; no man who has a broken leg or a broken arm; or he who is hunchback, or a dwarf, or who has a growth in his eye, or who has a boil-scar, or scurvy, or crushed testes." Maimonides explains the exclusion on the grounds that "most people do not estimate a person by his true form, but by his limbs and his clothing, and the Temple was to be held in great reverence by all." Somehow, for the Torah and Maimonides, one could be disabled and still function as the people's political leader, but one could not serve in the sacred precincts of the Temple. One verse in Deuteronomy even says that a man who has crushed testes or a severed penis "may not enter the congregation of the Lord"; it is not clear whether that only refers to a man who voluntarily maimed himself that way in service of some Canaanite god, or whether it refers to any man in that condition, and we also do not know the meaning or implications of "not entering the congregation of the Lord," but it clearly constitutes an exclusion of such men from normal status."

The Blemished Priest

Although a physical disability did not cause a person to lose his status as a *Kohen* (priest), it did disqualify him from performing the priestly functions. Physically defective priests were put to menial work about the Temple, such as cleaning the kindling wood from worms, for which a special area was set aside. In the book of Leviticus, there is a long list of physical attributes, which would disqualify the priest:

דַּבֵּר אֶל־אַהֲרֹן לֵאמֹר אִישׁ מִזַּרְעֲךָ לְדֹרֹתָם אֲשֶׁר יִהְיֶה
בוֹ מוּם לֹא יִקְרַב לְהַקְרִיב לֶחֶם אֱלֹהָיו: יח כִּי כָל־אִישׁ אֲשֶׁר־בּוֹ מוּם לֹא
יִקְרָב אִישׁ עִוֵּר אוֹ פִסֵּחַ אוֹ חָרֻם אוֹ שָׂרוּעַ: יט אוֹ אִישׁ אֲשֶׁר־יִהְיֶה בוֹ שֶׁבֶר
רֶגֶל אוֹ שֶׁבֶר יָד: כ אוֹ־גִבֵּן אוֹ־דַק אוֹ תְּבַלֻּל בְּעֵינוֹ אוֹ גָרָב אוֹ יַלֶּפֶת אוֹ
מְרוֹחַ אָשֶׁךְ: כא כָּל־אִישׁ אֲשֶׁר־בּוֹ מוּם מִזֶּרַע אַהֲרֹן הַכֹּהֵן לֹא יִגַּשׁ
לְהַקְרִיב אֶת־אִשֵּׁי יְהוָה מוּם בּוֹ אֵת לֶחֶם אֱלֹהָיו לֹא יִגַּשׁ לְהַקְרִיב:

Speak to Aaron and say: No man of your offspring throughout the ages who has a defect shall be qualified to offer the food of his God. No one at all who has a defect shall be qualified: no man who is blind, or lame, or has a limb too short or too long; no man who has a broken leg or a broken arm; or who is a hunchback, or a dwarf, or who has a growth in his eye, or who has a boil-scar, or scurvy, or crushed testes. No man among the offspring of Aaron the priest who has a defect shall be qualified to offer the Lord's gift; having a defect, he shall not be qualified to offer the food of his God.

(*Vayikra* 21:17-21)

The least bodily imperfection made one unfit for service in the Temple. While such a priest remained eligible to partake of the special priestly food he could not assume any of the public duties of the priesthood.

It may well be that this law reflected a common prejudice of associating one's character with his or her outer appearance and the necessity for the priest to inspire feelings or reverence and holiness in the people. Maimonides (a 12th century philosopher and expert in Jewish law) commented that the exclusion was due to the fact "that most people do not estimate a person by his true form, but by his limbs and his clothing, and the Temple was to be held in great reverence by all" (Guide to the Perplexed 3:45).

This point is elucidated in a more general way in *Sefer HaChinuch*, an anonymous 13th century work about the commandments:[vii]

Most human actions are accepted to those who see them according to the importance of the one who performs them. Thus, an individual who appears dignified and acts nobly will be viewed favorably in everything he does.... Therefore, it is fitting that the representative upon whom atonement depends should be one who is graceful, handsome, and becoming in all ways so that all may identify with him.

A blemish was viewed as an imperfection.

For Further Thought...

1. Why do you suppose that a person with a "blemish" would be forbidden from performing certain Temple rituals?

2. People fear what they do not understand. The fact that people with certain kinds of disabilities or "defects" cannot fully participate in some Temple rituals may be reflective of the fear that perhaps they could pass some "impurity" on to the sacrifice. How does this fear of the unknown extend to our lives today?

3. There was also a law prohibiting the sacrifice of a blemished animal. How, if at all, are the two related?

4. Does this change your view of how Judaism approaches disabilities?

5. Why did one have to be "perfect" to serve in the priestly role?

6. Do we have anything comparable to this today? What jobs have physical requirements that could be considered discriminatory?

Rabbi Bradley Artson, Dean of the Ziegler School for Rabbinic Studies at the University of Judaism offers a different interpretation of this text[viii]:

> "Certainly this passage, and others like it, lent biblical weight to the dehumanization of people with disabilities. Legislation in rabbinics confirmed that the blind, deaf-mute, and developmentally disabled were not allowed to participate as full members of Jewish society--either by functioning as acceptable witnesses in legal proceedings or as members of the minyan in religious services. While those prohibitions may have been reasonable in a time when no one could figure out how to educate or communicate with people with disabilities, the legacy those rules leave remains a tragedy in our day.

> "But there is another way of understanding this verse as well. Medieval commentators noted that precisely those traits which disqualify a kohen from performing his duties also disqualified an animal from being a sacrificial offering. Both the sacrifice and the one performing the sacrifice could not suffer from any mum, defect. At the same time, anyone, regardless of suffering those defects or not, was certainly welcome to bring a sacrifice to the Temple, and that sacrifice would be accepted by the kohanim, and would function to bring atonement between the individual and God.

> "In other words, both kohen and animal functioned not as representatives of human values and ideals, but rather as instruments in the Temple ritual. Just as you wouldn't use a broken hammer to build a house, the Torah insists that only

kohanim whose body can represent the typical Israelite (by virtue of its lack of any singular or distinctive traits) is a fitting implement for repairing God's relationship with Jewish individuals.

"*Midrash Va-Yikra Rabbah* picks up on this essential insight, and makes explicit that no one is disbarred from offering a sacrifice, regardless of their disability or handicap. To the contrary, God cherishes those who wrestle with their handicaps and have to make a greater effort to live their lives: said Rabbi Abba bar Yudan, "Whatever blemish God declared invalid in the case of a beast was declared valid in the case of a person. Just as God declared invalid in the case of a beast "one that was blind or broken," so God declared the same valid in the case of a person: "a broken and contrite heart, O God, you will not despise." In a very real sense, we are all handicapped, all of us disabled. Each of us balances personal weaknesses, inability's, injuries, working to compensate for them so they don't prevent us from living our lives to our fullest.

"In this regard, the *midrash*, and even this Torah portion remind us that only implements--like hammers, *kohanim*, and sacrifices--lack blemish. And only in them is a blemish a disqualification. For the rest of us, struggling to be decent, loving, and good, blemishes and disabilities are the catalysts that force us to wrestle with our own fears and inadequacies, and to grow."

Conclusion

Although specific examples can be cited of a connection between physical imperfections and divine displeasure, as in the cases of the curses in Deuteronomy (28:27-29) and the blemished priests, in general the biblical attitude toward the people with disabilities seems to be one of acceptance and protectiveness. It was not necessary, nor was it even desirable, for a great leader to be a physically perfect human being. In fact, the few examples of physical beauty and strength (such as Gideon or Samson) are fraught with questionable character traits. Even the exclusion of the priest from active service was due more to a caution about the people's perception of being a representative of God than to a negative view of his disability.

In comparing the *Tanakh* with other ancient literature, we find a refreshing openness to the notion that being physically imperfect, or having a disability, is yet another manifestation of the individuality which makes people different and unique.

Chapter Three—Rabbinic Literature

TERMINOLOGY

Halahic (legal) literature generally needs to operate with fixed definitions for any matter being considered. It is, therefore, quite specific in its classification of various disabilities. The following categories are most commonly mentioned in the sources of Jewish law and ones which we will discuss within this chapter:

- חֵרֵשׁ (*heresh*) one who can not hear (deaf) or can not hear <u>and</u> is without speech (*mute* in rabbinic terminology);

- אָלֵם (*ileim*) one who is without speech (*mute* in rabbinic terminology);

- שׁוֹטֶה (*shoteh*) one who has an intellectual impairment (retarded, or *insane* in rabbinic terminology);

- סוּמָא (*suma*) one who is without sight (blind);

- נִכְפֶּה (*nihpeh*), one who has epilepsy;

The two disabilities which are discussed most frequently in *Halahic* literature are those who can not hear or speak (in rabbinic terminology it has been traditionally referred to as the "deaf-mute") and mental retardation. It is not that these disabilities were necessarily more prevalent than the others, but they represented the conditions which were the greatest departure from "normal," from a legal standpoint.

DEAFNESS AND DEAF--WITHOUT SPEECH

Often in the Talmud and the legal codes, the person who can not hear or speak and one who is intellectually impaired are mentioned together with the minor as people who are legally incompetent and cannot be held responsible for their actions. The Talmud considers deaf/without speech to be not only a physical disability but a mental impairment as well. The general principle is expressed as follows:

חרש דלאו בר דיעה הוא

"A person who is deaf and nonverbal is not of sound mind."

It was the deafness, not the inability to speak, which led to the perception of incompetence, for, while one who is nonverbal was subject to certain legal limitations, these were the result of the particular disability and not a question of mental competence.

There is a discussion in the *Talmud* (*Shabbat* 153a-b) which categorizes various disabilities by degree. The case was about a person who was traveling on *Erev Shabbat*, before the beginning of Shabbat, and carrying various objects when darkness arrived. The question was what the person should do with the objects since it is forbidden to carry on Shabbat. The answer would depend on who was with him at the time to carry the object for him:

> **Mishnah:** If darkness comes when a person is on the road (on Friday evening), he entrusts his wallet to a non-Jew, but if there isn't a non-Jew with him, he places it on the mule. When he reaches the outer courtyard (where he is allowed to carry), he removes the objects which may be handled on the Sabbath, while

for those which may not be handled on the Sabbath (such as money or writing utensils), he unties the cords and the sacks falls off automatically.

If there isn't a non-Jew with him: (The Gemara continues, commenting on the phrase.) The reason (he places the wallet on the mule) is that there is no non-Jew with him, but if there *is* a non-Jew with him he must give it to him. What is the reason? As for a mule, you are under an obligation that it should rest (because one's animals also rest on Shabbat), but as for a non-Jew, you are under no obligation (to ensure) that he should rest.

We now consider a case in which he has several choices and must decide who will carry his wallet. The rabbis spend a great deal of time trying to establish which person should hold the wallet if the mule is not available:

(If there is) a mule, and one who can not hear or speak (*heresh*), someone who has an intellectual impairment (*shoteh*), or a minor—he must place it on the mule and not give it to the person who is a *heresh*, *shoteh* or minor. What is the reason? The latter are human beings whereas the former are not.

This seems obvious, but what about the situation in which there isn't a non-Jew or a mule:

(In the case of where there in only) a person who is both deaf and nonverbal (*heresh*) and someone who has an intellectual impairment (*shoteh*); (he must give it) to the person who is a *shoteh*; (in the case of where there is only) a person who is a *shoteh* and a minor—to the *shoteh*.

A person who has an intellectual impairment (*shoteh*) then, is considered to be in a lower category than someone who is both deaf and without speech (*heresh*) or a minor.

The discussion continues to establish a hierarchy between the person who is deaf/ nonverbal (*heresh*) who has an intellectual impairment (*shoteh*), and the minor in order to determine who is the most appropriate person to hold the wallet.

Since there is no difference between one who is a *heresh* (deaf/ non-verbal) and a minor (since neither are fully mentally competent in the eyes of the Talmud), perhaps there is another way to decide. We must consider other differences between the two, aside from their mental competence.

What then? Must he give it to the person who is deaf/ nonverbal (*heresh*) since the minor will (eventually) arrive at understanding?

Since the minor will eventually mature and arrive at a level of understanding, should he be on a higher level than the person who cannot speak or hear?

Or, perhaps he must give it to the minor, because the person who is deaf/ nonverbal (*heresh*) may be confused with an intelligent adult?

Since the person who is deaf/ nonverbal (*heresh*) appears more like a competent adult, he should be considered on a higher level. Therefore the wallet should be given to the minor so that people seeing this will not think that a competent adult is violating the laws of Shabbat. The Rabbis could not decide this issue and were split on their decision.

> ➤ **How do you feel about this discussion?**

> ➤ **Why do you think the rabbis perceived a person who is both deaf and without speech as having a mental impairment, and not just a physical disability? Was it the inability to hear or to speak that influenced that decision?**

EXERCISE

The rabbis in the Talmud were trying to determine which disability made a person less able to fulfill certain obligations. If you were asked to make such a priority list, how would you do it? For instance, try to classify the following disabilities in order of severity:

___ Blind	___ Intellectual impairment
___ Deaf	___ Nonverbal/ Without Speech
___ Uses a Wheelchair	___ Mental illness
___ Seizures	

There may appear to be some confusion in The Talmud regarding distinctions between combinations of deafness and the inability to speak. Originally, the intention seems to have been to disqualify someone who could not speak but could hear and someone who was deaf but could speak only on technical grounds in cases where hearing or speaking was an indispensable requirement. For instance, in the matter of serving as witnesses, the deaf (though able to speak) and the nonverbal (though able to hear) were still unfit to bear testimony because they could not meet the requirements based on *Leviticus* 5:1:

וְנֶפֶשׁ כִּי־תֶחֱטָא וְשָׁמְעָה קוֹל אָלָה וְהוּא עֵד אוֹ רָאָה אוֹ יָדָע אִם־לוֹא יַגִּיד וְנָשָׂא עֲוֹנוֹ׃

If a person incurs guilt when he has <u>heard</u> a public curse and—although able to testify as one who has either seen or learned of the matter—he does not give information, so that he is subject to punishment.

This verse was explained in the Talmud (Gittin 71a) as meaning that one must be able both to <u>hear</u> and to <u>speak</u>:

> Rav Zera said, "…it has been taught, 'If he does not give information (orally)' (*Vayikra* 5:1). This excludes someone who is nonverbal, since he cannot speak."

However, in cases other than testimony—where requirements were not as stringent and mental soundness was not in question—those who could hear or speak were not disqualified. A Mishnaic statement (*Terumot* 1:2) uses the term *heresh* in a limited sense, but defines it generally as referring only to one who is deaf-mute.

A _heresh_ who speaks but cannot hear may not give _terumah_ (witness statement), but if he does so, his _terumah_ is valid. The _heresh_ of whom the Sages generally speak is one who neither hears nor speaks.

Rashi comments on this use of the word _heresh_:

> A _heresh_ in our terminology is one who cannot hear. Our Rabbis, of blessed memory, also called one who is unable to speak (_ileim_) a _heresh_, since the cause of his inability to speak was deafness from the time he was still in the womb, thus having never heard the spoken voice, as has been described in the books of scientific questions… However, if one became deaf after having heard, or nonverbal after having spoken, then one may bring _terumah_.

A passage in the Talmud (_Hagigah_ 21B) supports this usage, which states that both the person who can speak but not hear (speaking-deaf) and the one who can hear but not speak (hearing-nonverbal) are to be considered as mentally competent in all matters:

> (Commenting on the phrase) Except a (_heresh_), _shoteh_ and minor, etc. (Our Mishnah) speaks of a _heresh_ in a manner similar to a _shoteh_ and minor: Just as the _shoteh_ and minor lack understanding, so _heresh_ (means) one who lacks understanding. This is in accordance with the statement we learned, "Wherever the Sages speak of _heresh_ (it means) one who can neither hear nor speak." This (would imply) that one who can speak but not hear, or hear but not speak is obligated. We have (thus) learned that which our Rabbis taught, "One who can speak but not hear is termed _heresh_; one who hears but not speak is termed _ileim_ (nonverbal). Both of these are considered competent in all that relates to them."

This source clearly makes a distinction between terminology and law. Although the term _heresh_ includes both one who is deaf and nonverbal, and the one who can speak but not hear, the law considers the latter to be competent in all matters, while the former is not. Is this distinction valid?

> ➤ **Should there be a distinction between a _heresh_ who is deaf and who is without speech and a _heresh_ who is able to speak?**

> ➤ **Is there any reason to think that we might consider this differently today?**

In the Jewish law codes, we shall see, this distinction is not made, placing all classes of _heresh_ into a more limited position.

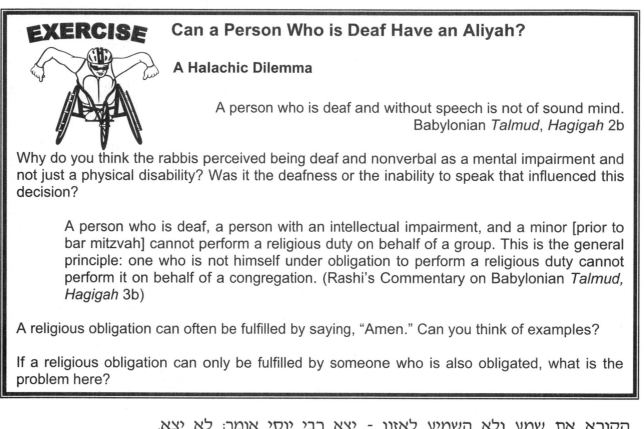

EXERCISE   **Can a Person Who is Deaf Have an Aliyah?**

A Halachic Dilemma

> A person who is deaf and without speech is not of sound mind.
> Babylonian *Talmud, Hagigah* 2b

Why do you think the rabbis perceived being deaf and nonverbal as a mental impairment and not just a physical disability? Was it the deafness or the inability to speak that influenced this decision?

> A person who is deaf, a person with an intellectual impairment, and a minor [prior to bar mitzvah] cannot perform a religious duty on behalf of a group. This is the general principle: one who is not himself under obligation to perform a religious duty cannot perform it on behalf of a congregation. (Rashi's Commentary on Babylonian *Talmud, Hagigah* 3b)

A religious obligation can often be fulfilled by saying, "Amen." Can you think of examples?

If a religious obligation can only be fulfilled by someone who is also obligated, what is the problem here?

הקורא את שמע ולא השמיע לאזנו - יצא רבי יוסי אומר: לא יצא.

If one recites the *Shema* without hearing what he says,
he has fulfilled his obligation. Rabbi Yose says he has not fulfilled it.
(Babylonian *Talmud, Brachot* 15a)

Based upon the text of the *Shema*, Jews are obligated to say the *Shema* twice a day. Why do you think Rabbi Yose holds that you need to hear the *Shema* in order to fulfill your obligation to say it?

> One must hear with one's ears what one utters with one's mouth, but if one did not hear, he still fulfills the obligation, as long as his lips utter [the words]. (*Shulchan Aruch, Hilchot Kriyaat Shema* 62:2)

➢ **What is the conclusion drawn by this text? Can a person who is without speech fulfill the obligation? A person who is deaf? A person who is both deaf and without speech?**

➢ **How might you relate this opinion to the fact that now many individuals who are without speech are able to communicate through various forms of sign language?**

➢ **Could a person who is deaf have an aliyah if he or she signed the brachot even if no one else in the room understood sign language because then no one would know when to say 'amen'?**

➢ **Would this prevent an individual who is deaf from becoming a Bar/Bat Mitzvah?**

MENTAL COMPETENCE, ILLNESS AND INSANITY

The mental competence of one who is deaf, nonverbal or even deaf and nonverbal, although assumed to have been impaired in varying degrees, was not viewed on the same low level as that of the *shoteh*—the intellectually impaired or mentally ill. Since the Rabbis recognized degrees of mental incapacity, the *Talmudic* definition of a *shoteh* is not at all precise. It seems to be more a matter of degree and judgment than exact specifications. There were certain forms of bizarre behavior which indicated a person's mental disorder or inability to think rationally, but the Rabbis ultimately had to rely on a combination of observation and judgment:

> Our Rabbis taught, "Who is (considered to be) a *shoteh*? One who goes out alone at night and one who spends the night in a cemetery, and one who tears his garments." It was taught: Rav Huna said, "(To be considered a *shoteh*, these acts) must all be (done) together." Rabbi Johanan said, "Even if (he does only) one of them." What is the case? If he does them in an insane manner, even (doing) one is also (proof). If he does not do them in an insane manner, does even (doing) all of them (prove) nothing? Actually (it is a case where) he does them in an insane manner. But if he spent the night in a cemetery, I might say that he did (it) so the spirit of impurity might rest upon him. If he went out alone at night, I might say that he was seized by lycanthrophy (a mental illness in which a person believes himself to be wolf). If he tore his garment, I might say that he was lost in thought. But as soon as he does all of them, he becomes like (an ox) who gored an ox, a mule and camel. (As a result) he becomes a *mu'ad* (a goring animal which had already been forewarned) in regard to all (animals). Rav Papa said, "If Rav Huna had heard of that which was taught, "Who is (deemed) a *shoteh*? One who destroys all that is given to him," he would have retracted (his view about what constitutes a *shoteh*)." The question was raised, "When he would have retracted, would he have retracted only with regard to the (case of the) one who tore his garment, because it resembles this (definition, of one who destroys things) or would he have retracted with regard to all of them?" It remains (undecided).
>
> (*Hagigah* 3b-4a)

> ➤ **Does the definition of mental illness bear any similarity to current standards?**

> ➤ **Why are the examples above chosen as indicative of mental illness?**

Maimonides, incorporating these criteria into law, was somewhat more specific and inclusive in his definition. He specifically mentioned monomania, a mental illness characterized by irrationality on one subject. His ruling is that a person who suffers from monomania is incompetent even in these matters about which he or she is rational:

> A *shoteh* is unfit to serve as a witness according to the Torah, because he is not obligated to observe the commandments. This does not mean only a *shoteh* who walks around naked and breaks dishes and throws rocks, but anyone who is sufficiently confused so that his mind is always irrational in one area, even though he may speak and inquire about other things. Thus he is unfit and considered a *shoteh*.
>
> (*Mishneh Torah, Hilchot Edut* 9:9)

Joseph Caro (16th century author of the *Shulhan Aruch*), in a work entitled *Kesef Mishneh*, sought to reconcile Maimonides' definition of *shoteh* with the Talmudic definition. Caro explained that Maimonides felt the cases used in the Talmudic passage (*Hagigah* 3b-4a) were cited only as examples, and were not to be taken as a complete definition of *shoteh*.

It seems clear from the sources that the Rabbis were quite willing to consider each case on an individual basis, since they understood that there were varying degrees of mental incapacity.

> ➤ **Where do you feel intellectual impairment would fit into this definition?**

> ➤ **Why was a *shoteh* considered not obligated to observe the commandments?**

Epilepsy

The Rabbis had difficulty in knowing how to deal with those who had epilepsy, since they did not understand the disorder. They considered those with epilepsy as sometimes lucid and sometimes insane:

> It has been taught, "If one is sometimes lucid and sometimes insane, when he is lucid he is regarded as sane in all matters, and when he is insane, he is regarded as insane in all matters.
>
> *(Rosh Hashana 28a)*

Maimonides was more exact in his definition, adding a warning that one with epilepsy had to be carefully examined before determining his or her legal status:

> During a seizure, one with epilepsy is unfit to give testimony, but when well, is acceptable. The same applies whether one is epileptic from time to time or one is always epileptic, with no set period. But this refers only to one whose mind is not always confused, for there are epileptics whose minds are confused even when they are not having a seizure. Therefore, we must be very careful with the testimony of someone with epilepsy.
>
> *(Mishnah Torah, Hilchot Edut 9:9)*

This is an area in which we have a better understanding than was available during the time of the Talmud.

> ➤ **Might our present day definitions reflect that understanding?**

> ➤ **Should a person who suffers seizures be treated any differently than one who does not?**

> ➤ **In what areas might a distinction be made?**

A Bar Mitzvah Ceremony for Children who are Intellectually Impaired
Schechter Institute of Jewish Studies, Written by Rabbi Reuven Hammer (OH 282:3)

Question: Is it permissible to hold a bar/bat mitzvah ceremony for one who is intellectually impaired?

Responsum: There are two ways of addressing this question: may a person who is intellectually impaired be called to the Torah? Or: is a person who is intellectually impaired a "bar mitzvah" in the *halahic* sense of being obligated to observe all of the *mitzvot*? We shall deal with the broader question because it includes the narrower question.

Technically speaking, the designation "retarded" is based primarily on intelligence tests: a child who scores one standard deviation below the norm is defined as "retarded." Thus, retardation is determined by the average intelligence of a given society and may therefore differ from one society to another and from one historical period to another. In practice, a person who is intellectually impaired is one who functions less effectively than most people in his society.

According to the *halahah*, minors are not obligated to perform *mitzvot*. Obligation to perform *mitzvot* begins at age 12 and one day for females and age 13 and one day for males (*Mishnah Avot* 5:21, *Niddah* 45b in the *Mishnah*). There are two categories of Jews who are exempt from performing *mitzvot*: a person who is both deaf and nonverbal and a "*shoteh*". In order to answer our question, we must define the term *shoteh*. According to *Hagigah* 3b a *shoteh* is a person who goes out alone at night, sleeps in the cemetery or tears his clothing. Another *beraita* says (ibid. 4a): "Who is a *shoteh*? He who destroys everything given to him". The *Shulhan Arukh* rules: A *shoteh* is "one whose mind becomes deranged and whose thoughts are constantly confused and disturbed: (Hoshen Mishpat 35:8). So too in *Tosefta Terumot* 1:3 we learn about a *shoteh* who is sometimes healthy and sometimes ill. Thus a *shoteh* refers to someone who has a mental illness, not an intellectual impairment.

But if a person who is intellectually impaired is not a *shoteh*, what is the *halahic* term for one who is intellectually impaired? Maimonides uses the word "*peti*" or simpleton to describe those "who do not understand things which contradict each other and who do not understand things the way other people do... such people are included among the *shotim*" (*Hilkhot Edut* 9:10).

Thus for the purpose of testimony, he includes the *peti* under the rubric of *shoteh*, but in other respects a *peti* is not like a *shoteh* and is obligated to perform all *mitzvot* (R. Joshua Falk, Sefer Me'irat Einayim to Hoshen Mishpat ibid.). Many modern rabbis concur (R. Simchah Bunim Sofer, R. Mosheh Feinstein, R. Chaim Pinchass Sheinberg, R. Shelomo Zalman Auerbach, and R. Eliezer Waldenberg). Therefore, child with an intellectual impairment who has reached the age of obligation who is able to study and recite the *Torah* blessings to God is a "*bar mitzvah*" and may therefore have an *Aliyah* and a *bar mitzvah* ceremony.

Chapter Four—
Jewish Law and People with Disabilities

INTRODUCTION

Until modern times, issues around disabilities were very different from today for many reasons and the law reflects that understanding. Today, we see things differently, and have different ways of adapting, understanding, and accommodating people with disabilities. In this chapter, we will begin with the pre-modern, rabbinical material not only to give a framework, but, understand its context. Then we will see how Jewish law today deals with these questions.

EXERCISE Look at the list below. What types of disabilities might have difficulty with some of the items on this list? Can you think of any other Jewish laws or customs that people with disabilities might have difficulty observing? At the end of this section, we will revisit this list to see how we can solve some of these issues.

ISSUE	Why would this be difficult and to whom?
Making pilgrimages to Jerusalem	**EXAMPLE:** People with mobility disabilities may find it difficult to navigate through certain historical sites.
Reciting *Shema*	
Sounding or hearing the *Shofar*	
Reading Torah	
Birkot HaShachar (Morning preliminary blessings)	
Tefillin	
Kissing a *mezuzah*	
Use of a wheelchair on Shabbat if there is no *Eruv*?	
Use of a motorized wheelchair or scooter on Shabbat?	
What if someone is on lifesaving equipment i.e. respirators and needs assistance on Shabbat?	
Use of crutches/canes and other adaptive devices on Shabbat?	

THE STATUS OF PEOPLE WITH DISABILITIES IN JEWISH LAW

Legal status is often determined more by technical requirements than by general attitudes, which often makes it difficult to detect any overall patterns or biases concerning people with disabilities in Jewish law. If, for instance, a person who is blind is deemed unfit to testify, it does not mean that the Rabbis were prejudiced against persons who are blind. Rather, in service to the strict demands of justice, certain requirements were established which were immutable. As we proceed to examine some (but not all) of the legal questions affecting the *people with disabilities*, let us remember to evaluate each case with legal minds and not jump to hasty conclusions based on our own attitudes.

 **EXERCISE** Divide into small groups, each one serving as a *Beit Din* (group of Judges). Consider the following series of texts and interpret questions about them (just like the ones that are answered in the book in the chapter "Jewish Law and People with Disabilities".

Rashi's Commentary on *Hagigah 3b (Babylonian Talmud)*: A person who is deaf, a person with intellectual impairment, and a minor (prior to *Bar Mitzvah*) cannot perform a religious duty on behalf of a group. This is the general principal: one who is not himself under obligation to perform a religious duty cannot perform it on behalf of a congregation. **A religious obligation can often be fulfilled by saying, "Amen." Can you think of examples? If a religious obligation can only be fulfilled by someone who is also obligated, what is the problem here?**

Brachot 15a (Babylonian Talmud) "If one recites the *Shema* without hearing what he says, he has fulfilled his obligation. Rabbi Jose says he has not fulfilled it."
Based on the text of *Shema*, Jews are obligated to say the *Shema* twice a day. Why do you think Rabbi Jose holds that you need to hear the *Shema* in order to fulfill your obligation to say it?

Shulchan Aruch, Hilchot Kriyat Shema 62:2 "One must hear with one's ears what one utters with one's mouth, but if one did not hear, he still fulfills the obligation, as long as his lips utter [the words]."
What is the conclusion drawn by this text? Can a person who is unable to speak fulfill the obligation? A person who is deaf? A person who is both deaf and unable to speak? How might you relate this opinion to the fact that now many individuals who are mute are able to communicate through various forms of sign language?

Could an individual who is deaf have an *aliyah* if he or she signed the *brachot* even if no one else in the room understood sign language because then no one would know when to say "amen"? Would this prevent people who are deaf from becoming *b'nai mitzvah*?

RITUAL LAW

The status of the _heresh_ and the _shoteh_ in Jewish ritual law is generally quite low. Based on the fact that people in those categories were considered to be mentally deficient, they were simply not obligated to observe the commandments, as Rashi comments on the definition of a _shoteh_:

> Who is considered to be a _shoteh_? One who is repeatedly referred to as one who is free from the commandments and any punishment, whose purchasing is invalid and whose selling is invalid.
>
> (Rashi on _Hagigah_ 3B)

Not being bound by (i.e., obligated to perform) the commandments, they could not perform religious duties on behalf of others:

> A _heresh_, a _shoteh_, and a _katan_ (a minor, someone who has not yet become a _bar/bat mitzvah_) cannot perform a religious duty on behalf of a group. This is the general principle: one who is not himself under obligation to perform a religious duty cannot perform it on behalf of a congregation.

The notion of performing an obligation on behalf of others may not be clear. It means simply that a person may fulfill an obligation by responding "Amen" to someone else fulfilling the same obligation. Most of the ritual legislation must be understood in light of the general rule—that only someone required to do something may exempt another person—even though there are exceptions.

> ➤ **A religious obligation can often be fulfilled by saying, "Amen." Can you think of examples?**

> ➤ **If a religious obligation can only be fulfilled by someone who is also obligated, what is the problem here?**

We shall now look at some of the ritual laws as they affect people with disabilities.

Recitation of _Shema_

In the Mishnah there is a disagreement over the validity of a person who is deaf reciting _Shema_:

> If one recites _Shema_ without hearing what he says, he has fulfilled his obligation. Rabbi Jose says he has not fulfilled it.
>
> (_B'rachot_ 15a)

A long discussion follows in the Talmud concerning the recitation of _Shema_. The very words of the _Shema_, "Hear, O Israel, the Lord our God, the Lord is One," may be problematic for a person who is deaf.

> ➤ **Based on the text of _Shema_, Jews are obligated to say the _Shema_ twice a day. Why do you think Rabbi Jose holds that you need to hear the _Shema_ in order to fulfill your obligation to say it?**

Some rabbinic authorities contended that it was not possible for a deaf person to fulfill the obligation of reciting *Shema*, because it could not be heard. However, in the Talmudic discussion. Rabbi Meir countered that argument by quoting a later portion of the same paragraph which says, "And these words shall be on your heart." Therefore, according to him, the intention of the heart—not the ability to hear—establishes the validity of *Shema*.

Two major codes of Jewish law reach a similar conclusion:

> One must hear what one says when he recites (*Shema*), but if he did not hear, he has nevertheless fulfilled his obligation.
>
> *(Mishneh Torah, Hilchot K'riyat Shema 2:8)*

> One must hear with one's ears what one utters with one's mouth, but if one did not hear, he still fulfills the obligation, as long as his lips utter (the words).
>
> *(Shulhan Aruch, O.H., Hilchot K'riyat Shema 62:2)*

In other words, one who can speak but not hear can recite the *Shema*. However, the complete *heresh* (one who is both deaf and unable to speak) and the *ileim* (one who is unable to speak) are exempt according to this view, since they cannot utter the words.

➢ **Do you think that literal "hearing" is more important or what is in one's heart?**

➢ **How might you relate this opinion to the fact that now many individuals who are unable to speak are able to communicate through various forms of sign language?**

➢ **What is the conclusion drawn by this text? Can a person who is not able to speak fulfill the obligation? A person who is deaf? A person who is deaf and unable to speak?**

➢ **How might you relate this opinion to the fact that now many individuals who are nonverbal are able to communicate through various forms of sign language?**

➢ **"Shema" is traditionally translated to mean "Hear". What if we translated the word "Shema" as "understand" or "focus"?**

Reading the *Megillah*

In order to qualify to read *Megillat Esther*, one must be capable of doing so on behalf of the congregation. Thus the Talmudic tractate dealing with the *Megillah* clearly states that the *heresh*, *shoteh*, and minor are not eligible:

> All are qualified to read the *Megillah* except a *heresh*, a *shoteh* and a minor. Rabbi Judah declares a minor qualified (to read).
>
> *(Megillah 19b)*

However, when this law was further developed in the law codes, there seems to have been some disagreement. Rambam (an abbreviation for the initials of Maimonides), on the one hand, mentions those who are ineligible, but he excluded the *heresh*:

> Both the reader and the one who hears fulfill their obligation as long as the reader is one who is obligated to read. Therefore, if the reader is a minor or a *shoteh*, one who hears him does not fulfill his obligation.
>
> (*Mishneh Torah, Hilchot Megillah* 1:2)

However, another major law code, the *Shulhan Aruch*, specifically mentions a <u>h</u>eresh as one who is not obligated:

> Both the reader and the one who hears it read fulfill their obligation, as long as (they) hear it read by one who is obligated to read. Therefore, if the reader is a <u>h</u>eresh or a minor or a *shoteh*, one who hears does not fulfill his obligation.
>
> (*Shulhan Aruch, O.H. Hilchot Megillah* 689:2)

The difference here is not whether a <u>h</u>eresh should read the *Megillah*—all agree that he should not. However, if he did, was his reading valid enough to fulfill the obligation for others or not? Rambam seems to feel that it is, while Joseph Caro (author of the *Shulhan Aruch*) is of the opposite opinion. We shall return to a related issue below—whether a <u>h</u>eresh can read from the Torah. For now, it should be noted that reading the *Megillah* involves the additional element of *pirsuma d'nisa*, "publicizing the miracle," in this case the miraculous deliverance of the Jews from Haman's schemes.

Recitation of the *Haggadah*

There was an opinion expressed in the Talmud that a person who is blind should be exempt from reciting the *Haggadah*:

> Rav Aha ben Jacob said, "Someone who is blind is exempt from reciting the *Haggadah*."
>
> (*Pesachim* 116b)

> ➤ **Why do you think Rav Aha ben Jacob would have made this statement?**

The discussion that followed outlines a debate concerning a person who is blind who does not have the ability to see and point out to his child the details of the Passover story. That view went against what another one of the Sages, Meremar, knew to be a case in which two great blind scholars—Rav Joseph and Rav Sheshet—recited the *Haggadah* in their own homes.

The argument continued, based upon the similarities and differences in usage of a few phrases and upon the question of whether the obligations under discussion were *d'oraita* (an obligation cited in the Torah) or *d'rabbanan* (founded on rabbinic interpretation).

Yet despite the complicated legal debates, the view finally accepted was that those with visual impairments may, indeed, recite the *Haggadah*. The precedents of the two learned, blind rabbis prevailed over the legal arguments. Their view is accepted, and a person who is blind may recite the *Haggadah*.

And according to the knowledge of the child his father instructs him.
(*Pesachim* 10:4)

> ➤ Why do you think that the precedent of Rav Joseph and Rav Sheshet reciting the *Haggadah* was given more weight than the legal arguments?

> ➤ Is there any difference between the reading of the *Megillah* and the reciting of the *Haggadah*?

Ritual Slaughtering: Sh'hitah

Of course we understand that a person who is blind could not serve as a *shohet* to slaughter an animal. Since minimizing the animal's suffering is of prime concern, one must see clearly to cut firmly and quickly. But what about the *heresh* and the *shoteh*, could either of them serve as a *shohet*? In their cases, the *Mishnah* prohibits their slaughtering on the grounds that they might err in some way, causing the animal to suffer and be non-kosher. Yet, there is some ground for permissibility:

> All may slaughter, and their slaughtering is valid, except a *heresh*, *shoteh* or a minor, lest they invalidate their slaughtering. But if any of these slaughtered while others were watching them, the slaughtering is valid.
>
> *(Hullin 2a)*

The reason that these individuals cannot slaughter is given in the *Gemara* (a further discussion of the *Mishnah*) and has to do with the precise manner in which ritual slaughter must be performed. Some of the technical requirements demand expertise in controlling the knife, including keeping it in continuous motion, forward and backward, without pause--*sh'heeyah*) or interruption until the cut is complete.

The law, as taught by Rambam, reflects the above discussion:

> A *heresh*, *shoteh* or minor, or a drunkard whose mind is confused, who slaughtered an animal—their slaughtering is invalid because they are not of sound mind and might err. However, if they slaughter before one who knows how and he saw that they did it correctly, then their slaughtering is acceptable.
>
> *(Mishneh Torah, Hilchot Sh'hitah 4:5)*

Thus, the issue is not entirely one's status as a *heresh* or *shoteh*, but one's competence to perform the task exactly as required.

Jerusalem Pilgrimage: *Re'iah*

The mitzvah of making a pilgrimage to the Temple in Jerusalem on the Festivals of *Pesah, Shavu'ot*, and *Sukkot*, was not encumbent upon all. It required both a sound mind and a sound body, indicating physical capability and mental awareness. The *Mishnah* lists the exceptions:

> All are obligated to appear (at the Temple), except a *heresh*, *shoteh*, and a minor, a person of unknown sex (*tumtum*), a person lacking sexual organs, women, unfreed slaves, one who is unable to walk, one who is blind, the sick, the aged, and one who is unable to go up (to Jerusalem) on foot.
>
> *(Hagigah 2a)*

The *Gemara* continues the discussion and further defines the requirement, depending on whether one could either speak or hear, or do neither:

> Ravina said (and according to others, it was Rava), "(The wording of this *Mishnah*) is defective and should read as follows: All are obligated to appear (at the Temple) and to rejoice, except a *heresh* who can speak but not hear, (or) hear but not speak, who is exempt from appearing. But, even though he is exempt from appearing, he is obligated to rejoice. Someone, however, who can neither hear nor speak, *shoteh* and a minor are exempt even from rejoicing, since they are exempt from all the precepts stated in the Torah.

"Rejoicing" refers to the sacrificial meal which was eaten or the offerings which were brought. Only the complete *heresh* (i.e., the person who was both deaf and unable to speak) was exempt from that as well. A *heresh* who could either speak or hear was exempt only from appearing, but was still required to "rejoice".

Even this law concerning the *heresh* was challenged in an important discussion about the ability of an *ileim* (someone who is unable to speak) to learn. The question was why someone who could hear or speak was exempt from "rejoicing." The discussion points out that one can learn without speech or hearing; however, the exemption was based on what was perceived to be an inability to "teach".

> Does this mean to say that someone who cannot talk cannot learn? But behold there were two men in the neighborhood of Rabbi (Judah) who were unable to speak….Whenever Rabbi (Judah) entered the college, they went in, sat down (in front of him), and nodded their heads and moved their lips. Rabbi prayed for them and they were cured. It was found that (from what they learned there) they were versed in Jewish law, *Sifra, Sifre*, and the whole Talmud!

> Two of the Rabbis disagreed about how to interpret specific words in the *Mishnah*, but both felt "teaching" was the issue. The details of the discussion are not as important for our purposes as the fact that the Rabbis acknowledged the capability of the deaf to learn and to understand. They were not, it is true, obligated to appear at the Temple, but that in no way reflected a belief that they were ignorant, only that one must be whole in body and mind to be under this obligation.

It is for this reason that one who was deaf in only one ear or blind in only one eye, or unable to use one foot was also exempt:

> Rav Tanhum said, "Someone who is deaf in one ear is exempt from appearing (at the Temple), for it is said (in the verse), "in their ears."…. Rav Tanhum said, "Someone who is unable to use one foot is exempt from appearing (at the Temple), as it is said, "*regalim* (literally, "feet")… Rav Johanan ben Dahabai said in the name of Rav Judah, "A person who is blind in one eye is exempt from appearing (at the Temple), for it is said, "*yir'eh* (He shall see)" and '*yera'eh* (He shall be seen).' Just as he comes to see, so he comes to be seen: as he comes to see with both eyes, so also to be seen with both eyes."

Although much of the explanation was based on the use of particular words in the *Tanakh*, this discussion also shows that the stress was on appearing "whole" at the Temple.

> ➢ Do you think it was fair to exempt these people from the mitzvah of Pilgrimage?

> ➢ What do you think the reason was?

Blowing the Shofar:

Again based on the general principle that only one who is obligated to perform a particular commandment can fulfill the obligation for another, a _heresh_, _shoteh_ and minor cannot blow the _shofar_ on behalf of the congregation. Moses Isserles (a 16th century codifier of Jewish law), further refined this law, excluding one who hears but cannot speak. His comment appears as an addendum in the _Shulḥan Aruch_:

> Anyone who is not obligated cannot act on behalf of others. A _heresh_, _shoteh_ and minor, are not obligated, and even if a _heresh_ can speak but cannot hear, he still may not do so because, not hearing, he is not obligated. **Addendum:** However, someone who hears but cannot speak can act on behalf of others.
>
> (_Hilchot Rosh Hashanah_ 891:1-2)

Another commentator, the Magen Avraham, commented that even if another person has to make the blessing for blowing the _shofar_, it is still valid. He also cited an important regulation that one who is blind is obligated for _tekiat shofar_. Since the obligation is to "hear" the _shofar_ (not to blow it) the _heresh_ is exempt, but this has no effect on a person who is blind. Here, again, we note the concept that, in general, a person's disability does not disqualify him from all areas, but only from those areas relating specifically to the disability.

Reading the Torah

We will deal with this issue in two parts, first relating to someone who is blind, and then to a _heresh_ (someone who can not hear or speak), since there are different legal concepts involved:

The Rabbis of the Talmud established the following principle:

> The written Torah must not be recited by heart.
> (_Gittin 60b_)

It was for this reason, explicitly, that the _Shulḥan Aruch_ forbade a person who is blind from reading the Torah:

> A person who is blind may not read (from the Torah) because it is forbidden to read even one letter by heart.
>
> (_Hilchot K'riat Sefer Torah, 139:4_)

It should be noted that this rule was written at a time when the custom was for each person called to the Torah to read from it. Later the custom changed so that it was acceptable for a "reader" to read from the Torah while the one called up (for an _aliyah_) only recited the blessings. It was, therefore, not necessary for him actually to see the Torah to do this. Thus, Moses

Isserles, in his note to this section, adopted a more lenient position, indicating that "now a person who is blind may read in the same way that we read from the Torah for an unlearned person (*am ha-aretz*)."

In a recent response adopted by the Committee of Jewish Law and Standards (January, 2003), Rabbi Daniel S. Nevins concluded "Jews who are blind should participate in synagogue rituals together with sighted Jews, all of whom are obligated to keep the Torah. Indeed it is in the interest of the Jewish community to include as many Jews as possible in the rituals of studying Torah and fulfilling *mitzvot*."

He noted that Jews who are blind may:
   a. Lead the congregation in prayer;
   b. Receive an *aliyah* and chant the appropriate blessings;
   c. Chant *haftarah*

He then suggests that:
   Because the Torah must be read for the congregation directly from a Torah scroll, and not from a printed text or from memory, Jews who are blind may participate in Torah reading in one of three ways:
   - By receiving an *aliyah* and chanting softly after the reader;
   - By serving as *meturgamon*, the verse-by-verse translator of a section of the *parashah*;
   - By reading from Braille a standard *maftir*, since it has already been chanted in the established fashion from the *Sefer* Torah.

He then adds the following interesting comment:

   Should new technology that allows blind people to read directly from the scroll become available, our options would expand. Meanwhile, these solutions all preserve our reverence for the sacred act of chanting Torah from a kosher scroll, while also allowing Jews who are blind to be included in the act of publicly accepting and revering the Torah.

Whether or not a _heresh_ can read from the Torah is a complicated question dealt with by the Beit Din of London in an extremely important *T'shuvah* (responsum), part of which is included in the section entitled, "Modern Legal Responses." The responsum deals with many of the laws we have been studying, including reading the *Megillah*, blowing the *Shofar*, and fulfilling obligations for others. The author of the responsum finds parallels with some situations and differences from others. The conclusion reached is that a _heresh_ may be called up to the Torah, recite the blessings and read from the Torah.

A MIRACLE *BAR MITZVAH*[ix]

Nearly 1,000 people crowded into the sanctuary at Syracuse, New York's Temple Adath Yeshurun on June 10, 1994 for Eyal Sherman's *Bar Mitzvah*. What was remarkable about this *Bar Mitzvah* is that Eyal has been a quadriplegic and ventilator dependent since the age of four. He cannot breathe on his own, walk, talk or eat. And yet, this remarkable young man learned to read Hebrew, mouth the words of his *Haftarah*, and attended the community Hebrew high school. Eyal attended *Shabbat* services every Saturday morning and was an active member of his Kadima chapter.

Eyal's *Bar Mitzvah* was made technically possible by using video cameras to project his picture on a large screen. Congregants watched the screen which showed both the text and Eyal's face, thus were able to follow along while he moved his lips. In the same way that most kids use microphones as a way to amplify their voices in large synagogues, the video cameras "amplified" Eyal's means of communication—his facial expressions and lip movements. This system worked so well that people responded to Eyal just as they would have at any other *Bar* or *Bat Mitzvah*. The utter silence with which Eyal mouthed his prayers was followed by the thunderous responding chant from the congregation.

Eyal's achievements reflect the courage and devotion of his family, friends, teachers, doctors, and the many others who believe he should be given all the love, support and opportunities possible. Because of this support, Eyal excels in his studies at a regular public school, plays third base on a baseball team for people with disabilities, and has been recognized as a "*Mitzvah* Hero" by USY and Kadima's Danny Siegel. His father, Rabbi Charles Sherman of Temple Adath Yeshurun described the *Bar Mitzvah* as an opportunity for the community to look through a window "to see something special, not something freakish".

The word "special" only begins to describe Eyal, who like most Kadimaniks gave a speech during his *bar mitzvah*…

"Shabbat Shalom*! Some people never thought I would have a* Bar Mitzvah *because I'm in a wheelchair and on a respirator. But this day proves them wrong! You might think this is like a miracle, when something happens that you don't expect. Here I am today on the* bimah *(pulpit), an honor and a pleasure to be where my father stands each week. I prepared for my* Bar Mitzvah *at home for a long time starting when I was very young. I've learned to say the* Kiddush, *blessing over the wine, and* Birkat Hamazon, *grace after meals. My family builds a* Succah *every year and we put on our ski jackets and eat in it. I learned the prayers by coming to services every Shabbat with my family. It was harder for me to prepare than other kids. The Cantor had to learn to read my lips.*

Having my Bar Mitzvah *means I am now a man and now my father can call me on the phone to help make up the minyan when they are short. The happiest part of this day is having my relatives and friends from all over America and Israel here with me.*

Even though my Bar Mitzvah *is different, or awesome or radical, being high tech, I never really thought about that.*

I just always knew that when I reached age 13, I'd be up here on the bimah *and have a* Bar Mitzvah *just like any other kid."*

Eyal's story has received plenty of media coverage, from local newspapers, Jewish publications, and even CNN. And yet beyond all of this attention there is a much more basic lesson to be learned. Eyal tells all of us that the word impossible is just that—impossible. Anything is possible; anything is within hand's reach.

Blessings before *Shema*

The blessings before the *Shema* are about light "...יוֹצֵר אוֹר, וּבוֹרֵא חֹשֶׁךְ"..." who creates light and makes darkness "יוֹצֵר הַמְּאוֹרֹת" . . . who creates lights". One might think that these blessings should be recited only by someone who derives benefit from light, thus excluding a person who is blind. This is discussed in the *Mishnah*:

> A person who is blind may repeat the blessings before the *Shema* and translate. Rabbi Judah says, "One who has never seen the light from his birth may not recite the blessings from the *Shema*.
>
> *(Megillah* 24a)

As often happens, the decision was reached as a result of life experience. In the ensuing discussion, Rabbi Judah's view was refuted by an observation of Rabbi Yossi:

> For a long time I was perplexed by the verse, "And you shall grope at noonday as the blind gropes in darkness" (Deut. 28:29). Now what difference does it make to a blind man whether it is dark or light? (I didn't find out) until the following incident occurred. I was once walking on a pitch black night when I saw a blind man walking in the road with a torch in his hand. I said to him, 'My son, why are carrying this torch?' He replied, 'As long as I have this torch in my hand, people see me and save me from the holes and the thorns and briars."
>
> *(Megillah* 35b)

Who could refute such dramatic testimony? Indeed, the *Shulhan Aruch (Hilchot Kriyat Shema* 69:2) follows the opinion of R. Yossi, stating that "A person who is blind, even one who has never seen the (heavenly) lights, recites the blessings before the *Shema* and recites "who creates the luminaries" since he benefits from the lights in that others can see and show him the way to go."

> ➢ **Why do you think R. Judah's opinion was that one who had never seen light should not recite the blessings before the *Shema*?**

> ➢ **Can you think of other ways, directly or indirectly, that some who is blind benefits from the light?**

Embracing the Darkness
Jacob Dov Artson

Barchu is a prayer we can say only in a *minyan*. There is great wisdom in starting our service by praising God together, because all Jews reflect a different face of God and so we really can't praise God fully unless we do it together in a group.

After the *barchu*, we praise God for creating light and darkness. I love that image because it means that both the triumphs and the failures are a praise of God since God creates both light and darkness, life and peace come from recognizing that all experiences, negative or positive, are an opportunity to be Godly.

I will try to always remember that even the darkness is a reflection of God's world so we don't have to fear it, we can embrace it as part of the journey of life in God's beautiful world.

From You Can Fly: Letting A Boy With Autism Speak for Himself
Selected Writings of Jacob Artson

Fringes: *Tzitzit*

The basis of the law of *tzitzit*—fringes that evidently used to be worn as part of one's clothing, but which now are on the *tallit*—is from *Bamidbar* 15:39:

וְהָיָה לָכֶם לְצִיצִת וּרְאִיתֶם אֹתוֹ
וּזְכַרְתֶּם אֶת־כָּל־מִצְוֺת יְהֹוָה

... look at it, and recall all the commandments of the Lord and observe them.

Even though a person who is blind is unable to see the fringes, he is nevertheless obligated to wear a *tallit* and to recite the blessing, for a reason similar to the reason for reciting the blessings before the *Shema*. Although the individual who is blind cannot see the *tzitzit*, others can see it, and this obligates him:

> A person who is blind is obligated (to put on) *tzitzit* even though he does not see it, since others can see it.
>
> (*Mishneh Torah, Hilchot Tzitzit* 3:7)

Leaders of Prayers: *Sh'liah Tzibbur*

The person who leads the congregation in prayer (the *sh'liah tzibbur*, literally, "representative of the community") must be able to act on behalf of the congregation and fulfill their obligations in the service. One who is blind could certainly fulfill this function, since he is obligated to pray. This is explained in the *Shulhan Aruch*:

> A person who is blind may go down to the stand (i.e., serve as *shaliah tzibbur*). However, he may not read from the *Torah*, because we are not permitted to recite by heart that which is written.
>
> (*Hilchot Birchot Hashahar* 53:14)

From this set of laws we can see how the Rabbis tried to open ritual participation as much as possible to those who are blind, except in cases where vision was explicitly required.

> ➤ **What can we learn about people with disabilities and ritual law in Judaism from the examples of the *tzitzit* and leading services?**

> ➤ **Given the laws and principles we have learned thus far, do you think a person who is blind could be a *hazzan*? What about being a rabbi?**

> ➤ **Try to imagine how other disabilities, such as "lameness" or intellectual impairment might be treated in Jewish law.**

CIVIL LAW-- *HERESH, SHOTEH* AND MINOR

Now that we have examined the status of people with disabilities in Jewish ritual law, we turn to questions of civil law.

In legal matters, the Rabbis often associated the *heresh* (one who is deaf and can not speak) with the *shoteh* (one of unsound mind) and the minor. The usual formulation, *heresh, shoteh, v'katan*, is abbreviated as חש"ו. All three categories are frequently considered to be of unsound mind for the purpose of legal matters, although it is clear that the Rabbis favored a closer connection between the status of a *heresh* and that of a minor. Even though the intentions of the *heresh* and minor may have been impossible to determine, nevertheless both were seen as capable of insight and limited understanding. We will now look at several categories in which the three are grouped together.

Possession: *Hazakah*

Hazakah is the right of ownership by virtue of possession for a definite length of time (depending on the object). If one held undisturbed possession as "an owner for a period of three consecutive years, without protest from the previous owner, the possessor's plea that he purchased the property or received it as a gift,"[x] is believed. However, for the *heresh, shoteh* and minor there can be no *hazakah*, either for their benefit or to their detriment. Since they are not considered to have sufficient understanding to realize that their property is in jeopardy, one cannot lay claim against it through the legislation applying to *hazakah*. On the other hand, even a three-year tenure doesn't entitle them to possession. Maimonides makes this point in a very concrete fashion, indicating that "even their eating of produce is not proof that the land is theirs, since they do not have a claim that the land should remain in their possession, but it returns to the owners."[xi]

Gifts: *Zeḥiyah*

Zeḥiyah is another form of possession in which one can acquire title by accepting a gift, either directly or by means of a proxy.

The *shoteh* and a minor who does not realize the value of an object cannot acquire title for themselves or for others; a *heresh* and a minor who is able to understand an object's value can acquire title for themselves, but not for others.

Even a *shoteh* and a minor who does not realize the value of an object may acquire gifts by means of an agent of sound mind. They 'acquire' the gift, but someone must do it for them. This is necessary, of course, in order to allow gifts to be made in a guardian-like transaction.

Sales: *Meḥirah*

In the matter of the validity of sales, the difference between a *heresh* and a *shoteh* is quite striking: a *heresh* may effect certain sales, but the *shoteh* may not:

> There are three (categories of people) whose purchasing is not valid and whose selling is not valid according to the Torah: the *heresh*, the *shoteh*, and the minor. However, the Sages ordained that the *heresh* and the minor could buy and sell in order to support themselves.
>
> (*Mishneh Torah, Hilchot Mehirah* 29:1)

Even here, however, there were stringent stipulations set down in order to validate such a sale. The transaction could involve only "movables," i.e., items other than property, and someone who conducted business by using gestures had to be examined to be certain of his competence. The use of gestures is defined in a *Mishnah*, where two different types of gesturing are mentioned:

> A *heresh* can hold a conversation by means of gestures. Ben Batayra says that he may also do so by means of lip-motions, if the transaction involves movables.
>
> (*Gittin* 59a)

To this Rashi adds that gestures with the hands are more reliable than lip motions.

The test suggested in the Talmud to determine whether or not one was of sound mind requires the individual to nod appropriately in answer to three questions. Although used here to see if someone is competent to effect a transaction, the procedure is based on the case of a man becoming mute after having asked for a get (bill of divorce) to be written:

> If he becomes unable to speak, and when they say to him, "Shall we write a get for your wife," he nods his head, he is tested with three questions. If he signifies "No" and "Yes" properly each time, then the get should be written and given.
>
> (*Gittin* 67b)

The nature of the questions was also considered in order to be absolutely sure that his gestures were not random and merely chance responses to the questions. Rashi, commenting on the

Talmudic discussion about the questions, suggested that the person should be asked if he wanted freshly picked fruit when it was out of season!

In the case of the _heresh_ effecting a sale, a further distinction was made between someone who was both deaf and could not speak and an _ileim_ (someone who could hear but not speak). In general, although there were certain restrictions, an _ileim_ could effect a sale, even a sale involving property. A _shoteh_, on the other hand, could not effect any sales at all, whether in movables or property, and the court had to appoint a guardian, just as in the case for minors.[xii] Finally, the case of someone with epilepsy was treated as being in between the _heresh_ and _shoteh_:

> As for one who is sometimes a _shoteh_ and sometimes of sound mind, like someone with epilepsy—when he is of sound mind, all of his actions are valid….like any other person of sound mind. But the witness must test carefully to make sure that the actions were not at the end or the beginning of a seizure.
>
> _(Mishneh Torah, Hilchot Mehirah 29:5)_

Legal Protections

In keeping with the biblical injunctions against placing " a stumbling block before the blind" and against "cursing the deaf," rabbinic law protects people with disabilities and warns against taking advantage of a person's disability.

A _Mishnah_ establishes certain rules which were made "in the interests of peace." Among these laws is one concerning objects found by a _heresh_, _shoteh_, or minor:

> (To take away) anything found by a _heresh_, _shoteh_ or a minor is considered as a kind of robbery, in the interests of peace. Rav Jose says, "It is actual robbery."
>
> _(Gittin 59b)_

Since these individuals could not legally acquire possession of an object, one could technically take it from them. This was, however, forbidden.

Another case involves goring by an ox owned by a _heresh_, _shoteh_, or minor. If an ox belonging to someone other than one of these three categories gored an ox that belonged to one of them, the owner of the goring ox would be liable. However, if the ox that did the goring belonged to a _heresh_, _shoteh_, or minor, a different law would apply. In that case, the court would appoint a guardian to be certain that a "warning" could be issues, and that the ox would be known as _mu'ad_, "forewarned". The difference from normal procedures, however, is that if the _heresh_ or _shoteh_ recovered—or when the minor became of age—the ox would no longer be considered "forewarned". In effect, then, the owner would get an extra chance. While those who were mentally incompetent were not completely free of responsibility, they were not expected to understand the various aspects of Jewish law. Thus, they were protected from law suits. If the situation required, a guardian was appointed to protect the interests of both people with disabilities and those who might suffer as a result of their legal immunity.

These laws were not meant to be the sole protection of people with disabilities; they were to serve as a general pattern to be followed in relating to people with disabilities. Both the interests of people with disabilities and the interests of society had to be protected, even though at times they might conflict.

> ➤ **What other applications of these laws, which would be applicable for our time?**

> ➤ **What other examples might there be where the interests of people with disabilities might clash with the interest of the rest of the society? Is there a point at which a protective society becomes "over protective" of the people with disabilities?**

Testimony: Edut

The Rabbis were quite strict in the matter of legal testimony. There could be no questions about the fitness of an individual to serve as a witness, because the testimony might affect the judgment. Here there were very few exceptions to the letter of the law:

A *shoteh* is unfit to serve as a witness by biblical law since he is not subject to the commandments. A *shoteh* does not mean only one who walks around naked and break things and throws stones, but anyone who is sufficiently confused so that his mind is always irrational in one area. Even though he may speak and inquire intelligently in all other matters, he is still considered a *shoteh* and his evidence is inadmissible.

> During a seizure, someone with epilepsy is unfit (to testify), but is legible when he is well. The same holds true for one who is epileptic from time to time or one who is always confused, for there are epileptics who, even when they are not having a seizure, their minds are confused. So we must be very careful with the admissibility of the testimony of someone with epilepsy.
>
> (*Mishneh Torah, Hilchot Edut* 9:9)

The *heresh* and the *ileim* alike were excluded from most testimony. The reason for this is hinted at in a *talmudic* discussion once again concerning the granting of a *get* (Jewish divorce document). The discussion revolved around the possibility of writing out instructions, rather than giving them orally. Interpreting Leviticus 5:1, a verse which deals with speaking in testimony, it was decided that one must be able not only to hear but to speak as well in order to testify.[xiii]

The sage Abaye noted that testimony is a particular legal institution with requirements stricter than any other. The only exceptional cases in which a *heresh* or *ileim* could testify were those in which a woman would otherwise become an *agunah*, woman whose husband was presumed dead or missing, but without proof:

> A *heresh* is like a *shoteh* in that his mind is not sound and he is not bound to observe the commandments. This applies to a *heresh* who speaks but does not hear as well as to one who hears but does not speak Even though testimony is given and his mind is sound, one must testify in court orally or be capable of oral testimony. And one must be capable of hearing the judges and the charge they address to him. Also if one lost his speech, even though they examine him in the manner that one is examined for a get and his testimony is found to be cogent and he testifies in writing, it is not valid at all, except in cases involving *agunah*, in which event the Rabbis favor leniency.
>
> (*Mishneh Torah, Hilchot Edut* 9:11)

Thus we find that except in the case of the *agunah*, the Rabbis wanted to be absolutely sure that any witness would both understand what he had seen and would have the ability to communicate that testimony clearly.

> ➤ **How might modern developments regarding the deaf effect these laws of testimony?**

> ➤ **Why were the rabbis more lenient when the case was one of agunah?**

Marriage and Divorce

The Rabbis felt that a *shoteh* could not be married, for marriage requires the recitation of certain formulae and the full and knowledgeable consent of both parties. However, they accepted such marriages between *her'shim*, enabling them to enjoy as normal a life as possible and to experience the pleasures of having a family. The *shoteh*, on the other hand, being totally of unsound mind, like a child, could not marry.

These laws are based on an extensive section in the Talmud dealing with laws of marriage, divorce, and Levirate marriage. (That was the obligation to marry one's sister-in-law if one's brother died without children, enabling the family to continue the brother's name.) The Mishnah begins by explaining how a *heresh* could marry and divorce in such a situation:

> A *heresh* who married a woman of sound senses or a man of sound senses, who married a *hereshet* may, if he wishes to release (divorce) her, do so, and if wishes to retain her he may also do so. As he marries (the woman) by gestures so he divorces her by gestures.
>
> (*Yevamot* 112b)

The Rabbis also questioned the difference between a *heresh* and a *shoteh*. Why could the former legally enter marriage while the latter could not? Their explanation centered around the likelihood of a happy marriage:

> (In the case of) a *heresh* (man or woman), where the rabbinical ordinance could be carried into practice, the marriage was legalized by the Rabbis; (in that of) a male or female *shoteh*, where the rabbinical ordinance cannot be carried into practice—since no one could live with a serpent in the same basket (i.e., it would be very difficult to live with someone of unsound mind)—the marriage was not legalized by the Rabbis.
>
> (Yevamot 112b)

This source seems to involve a value judgment and advice rather than any legal restrictions. In other words, one could marry a *shoteh*, but the marriage would have no legal standing. Nevertheless, such a marriage could be a happy one, blessed with love and children.

Honor and Degradation

According to Jewish law, one who is insulted in public has the right to monetary compensation for the disgrace. How does this law apply to people with disabilities? According to the *Talmud* (*Bava Kama* 86b), someone who is blind, someone who is deaf and cannot speak, and a minor are all subject to degradation. They are, therefore, entitled to compensation for an insult. Only a *shoteh* is not subject to be paid for degradation, and the reason is startling:

It may be said that the *shoteh* by himself constitutes a disgrace which is second to none.

In other words, one who is already disgraced to such a degree is not subject to further degradation. The *heresh* and one who is blind, although with a disability, are not considered to be beyond insult are, therefore, entitled to compensation.

However, there is another interpretation of this law and it focuses on the one who is doing the insulting or humiliation. According to this interpretation, it is not that the *shoteh* cannot be disgraced, but rather that the *shoteh* cannot be held liable for insulting behavior, since he or she cannot know the effects of the insult.

> **How do you react to the manner in which this law treats the shoteh?**

> **Is there any class of people that should not be entitled to compensation for disgrace and insult?**

> **How do you react to the manner in which it treats those with other disabilities?**

Conclusion

It can be seen from the examples given, that the *heresh*, *shoteh*, and minor have very little legal standing in Jewish codes. They are not considered to be responsible agents, nor are they liable for damage they cause others, while others are responsible and liable for damage to them or to their property. Their claims are generally not heard nor are the claims of others against them. They do not take oaths nor do others take an oath on their account.

Since most of these legal decisions are based on an assumption of mental incompetence, we find many distinctions made between the *heresh* and *shoteh*, and the *heresh* and the *ileim*, except, of course, in the area of testimony.

Since the time that these legal decisions were made, we have learned a great deal more about these disabilities. People who are without speech no longer lack the ability to communicate. The rabbis somewhat understood this, but did not have the same understanding that we have today.

THE BLIND: SUMA

Those who are blind are regarded quite differently from the *heresh* and *shoteh*. Although Rabbi Judah expressed the opinion that the blind should be exempt from all of the *mitzvot*, even he admitted that this would be a purely legal exemption, but not an exemption in fact:

> And likewise Rabbi Judah exempted him (the person who is blind) from all the commandments … It appears that even though Rabbi Judah exempted a person who is blind from all of the commandments, nevertheless, by rabbinic enactment, he is obligated....because if a person who is blind were to be exempted even from rabbinic enactments, he would be as a non-Jew who is not guided by the Torah of Israel at all.
>
> (*Tosaf., Bava Kama* 87a)

The Rabbis understood that those who were blind didn't have mental limitations as a result, though they didn't realize that the same was true for the _heresh_. The only legal restrictions imposed are directly related to their blindness.

Testimony

One who is blind cannot serve as a witness since they cannot testify that they have seen a person or an act. Here again the rules of testimony are particularly severe and no exceptions are made to this rule:

> People who are blind, even though they may recognize a voice and know the parties, are still unfit (to testify) according to the Torah, as it is written, "And he is able to testify, and saw......" (Lev. 5:1), meaning that one who is able to see is able to testify. One who is blind in only one eye is fit to testify.
>
> (_Mishneh Torah, Hilchot Edut_ 9:12)

> **Consider** if you think it is reasonable to reject the report of someone who is blind, especially in a system, which requires precise transmission of quotations, including the names of speakers.

Serving as Judges

A general principle is set down, excluding the blind from serving as judges. The rule equates the qualifications for witnesses with those for judges, making the latter even more stringent:

> **Mishnah:** Whoever is eligible to act as a judge is eligible to act as a witness, but one may be eligible to be a witness and not a judge.
>
> (The **Gemara** comments on that statement): What (did this intend) to include? Rabbi Johanan replied, "To include one who is blind in one eye."
>
> (_Niddah_ 50a)

➤ **What might be the reasons for such restrictions?**

➤ **Why do you think blindness is not regarded in the same degree as deafness? Might it be because blindness was so much more common, especially among the elderly?**

Delivery of a Get

A person who is blind cannot act as the bearer of a get from foreign lands, because he cannot comply with the technical requirement of declaring. "It was written and signed before me (in my sight)." The Mishnah (Gittin 23a) lists a number of people ineligible to bring a get, including a _heresh_, _shoteh_, minor, some who is blind, and a heathen. The point is made there that whoever delivers a get must be of sound mind when receiving the get and when delivering it. If he is "impaired" at one of those times, he may not deliver it. Conversely, if he was "impaired" at a time other than when he received the get and he delivered it, he is eligible. However, what does this have to do with a person who is blind, who is always considered to be of sound mind? A humorous discussion follows between Rabbi Sheshet and Rabbi Joseph:

We understand a _heresh_, _shoteh_, and a minor being disqualified (from delivering a get, because they are not of sound judgment; also a heathen, because in any case he himself cannot give a get (to his wife). But why should a person who is blind be disqualified?

R Sheshet says, "Because he does not know from whom he has taken (the get) and to whom he delivers it." R Joseph strongly disagreed. In that case, (he said,) "how is it permitted for a man who is blind to associate with his wife, or for any men to associate with their wives at night time? Isn't it by recognizing the voice? So here, (a person who is blind) can recognize the voice?" "No," said R Joseph; "the fact is that here we are speaking of (a get brought from) foreign parts, (the bearer of which) has to declare, 'In my presence it was written and in my presence it was signed,' and a blind man cannot say this."

(_Gittin_ 23a)

EXERCISE

What conclusions can you draw from the Jewish legal sources above?

What do you feel was the tone of the rabbis towards those with disabilities?

On a scale of 1-10, how sympathetic do you feel the rabbis were to people with disabilities?

Not very sympathetic   Very Sympathetic
1   2   3   4   5   6   7   8   9   10

Why did you choose the number that you did?

What did you feel were the most positive laws that were discussed in this chapter?

Which ideas made you feel most uncomfortable?

CONCLUSION

We can now draw several conclusions:

1. Legal sources are not necessarily the sole, or even the best barometers of attitude, but they do afford insight into the way people with disabilities were viewed at various times.

2. Mental disabilities—or, at least those disabilities which were viewed as having a component of mental limitation, such as a _heresh_ and _shoteh_—were much more disabling than physical disabilities (such as being blind or unable to walk). Individuals with one of the mental disabilities had little or no standing in Jewish Law, while the latter were disqualified only as a specific outcome of their disability.

3. The law demanded fairness and protection for people with disabilities, that they should not be taken advantage of nor held responsible for anything beyond their control.

4. Distinctions were made between levels of disabilities, particularly those concerning mental soundness. Testing procedures were devised to determine each individual's level of functioning.

Regarding this last point we must add one final note: Much of our conception and understanding of people with disabilities today is quite different from what it was in _talmudic_ times. Today, many of the hearing impaired and deaf can beautifully communicate by signing and by speaking. People who are blind can learn and participate in the world in ways never dreamed of by our ancestors. People who can not walk can ambulate by new means and those without any ability to use their arms or legs, too, are frequently able to function in a productive and positive way.

Perhaps, as Herbert Schwartz suggests, the leadership of the Jewish community should be seriously considering changes in some of our legal regulations in light of these new developments:[xiv]

> One may argue that the Rabbis did not belabor the apparent inability of the congenitally deaf to learn. At times, it was made explicit that the deaf were excluded from certain tasks due to insufficient intelligence; as with the minor, so with the deaf. While the reason for the law was specific, the law itself was general; a minor (or deaf person) may be exceptionally intelligent, yet he or she will form no exception to the law.

The Rabbis were unable to satisfactorily determine the intent of the person who is deaf before them—and this barrier was at the root of their attitude toward the deaf. Biblical verses were used to exclude written testimony of one who became deaf not because he could not reason (he had already mastered the skill of writing), but because a man writing out his answers to his cross-examiner had time to think and formulate his answer, thereby clouding his original intent. Some Rabbis went so far as to say that the actions of the deaf were valid, the intentions of the deaf, invalid.

However, today communication with the deaf has changed dramatically. There are several teaching methods which are employed effectively, depending on the severity of the disability and the orientation of the institution involved. In general, the various techniques for teaching those with hearing impairments, and for teaching them how to communicate fall into two groups:

visual or auditory.[xv] Visual methods include the use of manual alphabets and signs as well as blackboards and paper. Auditory methods, often used with the partial or residual hearing that someone with a hearing impairment may have, include speech and lip reading and similar systems. Although, as Schwartz notes, "deafness retards the development of verbal language...the average deaf person today has the wherewithal to conduct his public as well as his personal affairs."

Modern legal opinion has indeed begun to take account of these changes. In the next few pages we will look at just a few attempts to deal with some difficult legal problems and raise some of the issues which still like ahead of us. These challenges to us are summed up by Rabbi Schwartz:[xvi]

> The deaf are now a responsible group for all intents and purposes, and deserve the acceptance of their community. We must seriously consider including the deaf (both oralists and finger-spellers), in a hearing minyan and allowing the deaf an aliyah in a hearing synagogue (including the man who lost his hearing after his minority, and more important the man who is congenially deaf and has learned to use his voice). We must permit substitute forms of communication required by the normal interplay of the deaf in a hearing world in all legal matters. We can no longer wait for "a time when God will unstop the ears of the deaf."

The legal disabilities of the deaf who are unable to speak are entirely due to the emotional drain resulting from their inability to communicate audibly with their environment. But in view of the modern advancement in the treatment of such cases, it has been suggested that their religious and legal status may now be modified

MODERN LEGAL RESPONSES

Now we will raise several interesting and difficult legal questions, some of which have been faced and some which will continue to receive attention. These, however, are samples. No doubt as you read about these issues others will occur to you. It should also be pointed out that the body, which decides law for the Conservative Movement, is the Rabbinical Assembly Committee on Jewish Law and Standards. Those matters cited here from other sources are brought at least as much for the questions as for the solutions, although several items from the Law Committee do appear at the end of this chapter.

Mezuzah

A Mezuzah is traditionally placed within the upper third of the doorpost, making it inaccessible to the young and people confined to wheelchairs. Danny Siegel posed a question to his teacher:

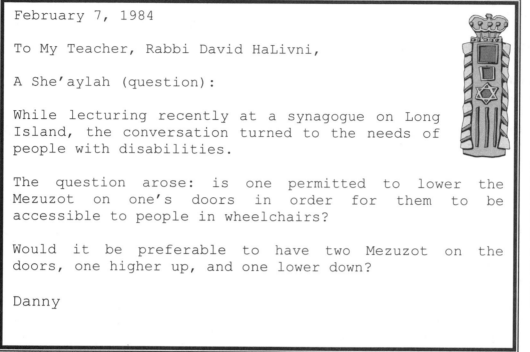

February 7, 1984

To My Teacher, Rabbi David HaLivni,

A She'aylah (question):

While lecturing recently at a synagogue on Long Island, the conversation turned to the needs of people with disabilities.

The question arose: is one permitted to lower the Mezuzot on one's doors in order for them to be accessible to people in wheelchairs?

Would it be preferable to have two Mezuzot on the doors, one higher up, and one lower down?

Danny

Rabbi HaLivni's answer is direct and powerful:

It would be preferable to lower the Mezuzah if it is obvious that it was done so for the sake of people with disabilities.

➢ **How might one lower the mezuzah to make it obvious that it was lowered for the disabled?**

➢ **Are there any other ritual objects which might also have to be changed?**

Mikvah

According to Jewish law, a person who uses a mikvah (ritual bath) must not have any barriers between oneself and the water. A physically handicapped woman who cannot stand alone has had a major problem with this. In Jerusalem, where it is estimated that approximately two hundred disabled, observant women live, a special mikvah is being constructed.

Since the first publication of this sourcebook a number of mikvaot have been constructed that are completely or at least partially handicapped accessible. Of those that are not completely accessible, there is at least a ramp as well as wheelchair accessibility in the mikvah facility, the chair is not necessarily able to go into the mikvah itself.

Shabbat

Another case is brought concerning Shabbat observance.[xvii] In an extremely religious seminary on a Shabbat, a young lad with crutches attempts to descend the stairs:

> At this point, a young lad sallies forth from the study hall, and grasps the rails, intending to start down the stairs. He tries to transfer his spare crutch from his right hand to his left. Instead, he manages to lose both. They go clattering down the first staircase, and, bouncing off the walls make their way almost to the first floor before stopping. The young man, not knowing what conduct most befits his situation, sits down on the stairs and begins to cry.

Two opinions are voiced. One is that since the crutches are forbidden to be handled on Shabbat by anyone but the user, and since the boy's life was not in imminent danger, he could stay upstairs until after Shabbat.

But another view was expressed and acted upon:

> "If the Talmud forbids us to taunt the lame and the impaired." They held, "so much more does it forbid us to celebrate the holiday while this young man sits crying on the stairs." And, with this, the youngest of the Bobovers (the students), being the most nimble and the first to reach the crutches, picked them firmly in his grip and brought them to the third floor.

Now it is true that the young man's life wasn't in any danger, and ordinarily the use of possession of the crutches would be forbidden on Shabbat to all but him. But there are more complicated questions related to this issue. What if a person with a disability using crutches or a wheelchair needs help on Shabbat? What about a malfunctioning respirator for an victim of emphysema?

These and other similar questions of potential Shabbat violation are on a delicate balance which must weigh the needs of often conflicting priorities

> ➤ **What other issues of a similar nature can you think of?**

Reading Torah

Writing a responsum for the London Beit Din, Aryeh L. Grossnass considered "The Issue of Reading the Torah by a Person who is blind."[xviii] He brings many of the pros and cons, concluding finally that a _heresh_ may be called up to read from the Torah.

Grossnass considers analogies with other legal precedents, especially with reciting the _Shema_ and with someone who has a temporary hearing impairment. He then summarizes the reasons for permitting a _heresh_ (who can speak) to celebrate his Bar Mitzvah by reading from the Torah:

> And therefore, according to the law in our case we can call a _heresh_ to the Torah for his Bar Mitzvah, to recite the blessings and to read his Torah portion..... Nevertheless with reading the Torah, whose entire obligation is the public study of Torah even though it must be from the scroll, we do not require one's hearing oneself. And as for the blessings for the Torah, he can also recite them even though from the outset he should be able to hear himself, yet since the Torah

blessing is mainly for the honor of the congregation, he might not even have to fulfill their obligation but simply recite the blessing for his own reading. And, regarding his obligation, since he cannot possibly hear, it is as if he fulfilled it after the fact although he could not hear himself. Even if we say that the congregation must fulfill their obligation by hearing the blessing, certainly they can do this with the others who come up.

➢ **Although the manner in which the decision was reached entails much technical material, can you accept the decision?**

➢ **What factors would you include in making decisions of this nature?**

THE MIRACLE OF TODD'S BAR MITZVAH [xix]

In my job, I attend many bar and bat mitzvahs of children with special needs and all of them touch me deeply. Recently I attended one which affected me even more.

Todd is a handsome 13-year-old who is autistic, non-verbal, skinny and gangly...and a bundle of nerves. He seldom sits when he can pace; he squeezes the fingers on one hand to the point of misshaping them; he screams and shrieks and, when most frustrated, spits in the other person's face. In the absence of speech, Todd demands attention in every other way. He uses "facilitated communication" with a small group of adults as well as using a very sophisticated Pegasus laptop computer with voice synthesizer.

Todd attends a self-contained class in middle school during the week; on Sundays, he participates in the special education program at Temple Chai, in Phoenix, Arizona. His teacher Arleen has a class of half a dozen students whose disabilities include autism, Down Syndrome, developmental and physical disabilities. Half of the students are non-verbal, yet Arleen has taught them about Jewish holidays, Shabbat (the Sabbath), mitzvot ("good deeds") and tzedakah (acts of charity). Using constant repetition for reinforcement and a multisensory approach which includes baking challah (egg bread) for Shabbat, decorating Seder plates for Passover, learning the blessings as they eat their snacks and much more, these children who everyone assumed could never participate in their religious activities have embraced the rituals of their families.

But could these severely impaired students who had little or no English vocabulary learn to read or write or speak Hebrew, the language of Jewish prayers and study? Undaunted by the challenge, Arleen introduced the chanting of prayers within the structure of her weekly class. She recognized in Todd an eagerness to learn more, and so Arleen taught him the Hebrew alphabet. Soon Todd could point to letters she picked at random! Arleen taught Todd words in Hebrew; again, he could pick them out of a page of written Hebrew. Todd worked his way up to phrases and sentences of the traditional prayers. And so they began to prepare for his bar mitzvah...

Having known Todd most of his life, my greatest concern was his inability to sit or stand still for any period of time. Even when he was watching his favorite videotapes, Todd bounced and rocked and paced with an overabundance of energy. When he attended Shabbat or holiday services at the synagogue, he rarely stayed more than 20 or 30 minutes before his noise became too disruptive. My other concern was that Todd might panic and obstinately refuse to "perform" his parts of the bar mitzvah service. His parents, the rabbi and I talked seriously about "alternate plan B" should either of those things occur.

The day of Todd's bar mitzvah arrived. Todd's teacher, therapists and parents had worked for months to prepare him for the 90 minutes ahead of him. The computer had been programmed with prayers and his Torah portion; the volume level for the voice synthesizer was checked and re-checked. Todd looked at himself in his new sportcoat and dress shirt and facilitated to his mother, "I look really good; I hope everyone else dresses up, too!" As the service started, Todd took his seat on the bimah (stage) next to his teacher. The 140 congregants held their collective breaths to see what Todd would do, and he amazed them all. Gone were the shrieks and the pacing, the intense nervousness and physical roughness. In their place was a sense of calm and serenity. Todd stood and sat throughout the service, poised to press the screen of his computer for prayers and prepared to carry the small Torah in the procession around the sanctuary. His electronically-generated speech at the end of the service included words of thanks to his teachers and his family and all the friends whose faith and confidence in him brought him to this day. Todd was the very picture of dignity and composure.

The rabbi, like everyone else in attendance, was fighting back tears as he spoke. Rabbi William Berk spoke of Todd's lesson to us all, that there is a mystery in silence, but there is also a message. Todd "spoke" to us through his silence, teaching us that we must respect each and every person regardless of his capability or disability, and we must listen to them in so many different ways. Rabbi Berk praised Todd's teachers and all of the people who helped Todd and his family reach this moment in their lives, and he remarked on how blessed we all were to be allowed to share it.

Miracles do happen, and I think I witnessed one that day. If you are curious about the lasting effects of Todd's restraint and composure, I can share with you the follow-up story. My family attended a celebration at Todd's home that evening. Todd and my son Joel (who also has autism but is able to speak) were in the bedroom, as usual, arguing (in their own manner) over which videotape to watch. Todd was back to pacing and shrieking, squeezing his fingers and fiddling with the TV, eight hours after his bar mitzvah. Oh, but for those magical 90 minutes earlier in the day, Todd was at peace.

Used with Permission from Becca Hornstein, Council for Jews with Special Needs, Phoenix, AZ

QUESTIONS TO CONSIDER

We conclude this chapter with a list of a few of the questions recently addressed to the Rabbinical Assembly Committee on Jewish Law and Standards. Questions are sent to the Committee from Conservative rabbis all over the world.

> ➤ A woman is married to someone who has been committed to a mental institution. They were married for several years before his disability became obvious. Since a man must be mentally competent to grant a divorce, can the woman obtain a divorce according to Jewish law?

> ➤ A fifteen year old boy, blind from birth, read a *haftorah* for his Bar Mitzvah from Braille. He now wants to learn how to read the Torah. May he read Torah from braille?

> ➤ A woman, now converting to Judaism, wants her 16 year old son to be converted, as well. The boy has Down's Syndrome, and the intellectual capacity of a five year old. Can the boy be converted, assuming a conversion require one's consent and knowledge?

➢ May a seeing-eye dog be brought into a sanctuary or onto the *bimah*?

➢ We have looked at but a few of the many questions which have been or should be raised. Perhaps we can, from our own experiences, think of other issues which might need review and which cry for change.

EXERCISE

Look at the list below from the beginning of this chapter. What solutions were mentioned in this chapter? What other solutions can you come up with?

ISSUE	POSSIBLE SOLUTION
Making pilgrimages to Jerusalem	
Reciting *Shema*	
Sounding or hearing the *Shofar*	
Reading Torah	
Birkot HaShachar (Morning preliminary blessings)	
Tefillin	
Kissing a *mezuzah*	**EXAMPLE:** Lowering the mezuzah so that people in a wheelchair can reach it.
Use of a wheelchair on Shabbat if there is no *Eruv*?	
Use of a motorized wheelchair or scooter on Shabbat?	
What if someone is on lifesaving equipment i.e. respirators and needs assistance on Shabbat?	
Use of crutches/canes and other adaptive devices on Shabbat?	

Chapter Five—Attitudes in the Midrash

THE WORLD OF THE MIDRASH

Having examined various legal sources which deal mainly with practical considerations of being disabled, we now turn to the world of the *Midrash* or *Aggadah*. It is a world of freedom, a world in which the Rabbis were not restrained by the strictures of practicality and legality.

From the *midrashic* material, we will see the Rabbis struggling to understand the causes of various impairments, to find some meaning for what they saw as the suffering of people with disabilities. What they conclude may not always be what we would conclude, but it is important for us to enter their world, to experience their perspective and understand their purposes. It is only in this way that we will be able to fathom the depths of Jewish attitudes and sensitivity.

Midrash is, essentially, "interpretation." It is rooted in the *Tanakh*, and it is the biblical text which it interprets. Yet, more often than not the biblical connection is merely a means to express a particular point of view or to teach a lesson. *Midrash* was, in fact, the rabbinic sermon, tied to the text, yet free to wander.

Since the Rabbis often had differing opinions, and since attitudes on most important topics are not monolithic, we may find *Midrashim* which seem to contradict each other. This does not necessarily mean that one is "right" and the other "wrong"; it simply means that life is complex and our attempts to understand it must reflect that complexity. We can learn from an interpretation and its opposite. Each has something to teach. If we can grasp this, then we are ready to enter the world of *Midrash*.

THE CAUSE OF DISABILITIES

Isaac's Blindness

There are several biblical accounts in which people are blinded. The *Midrash* tries to explain the causes of the blindness, although the explanations are often more in the nature of moral lessons. Numerous possibilities may be offered, each with its own particular lesson in mind. In the following *Midrashim* we can find no less than six reasons for Isaac's blindness.

> Isaac was made prematurely old by the conduct of his daughters-in-law, and he lost his sight. Rebekah had been accustomed to the incense burned before idols in the home of her childhood and could therefore bear it under her own roof. Unlike her, Isaac had never had any such experience while he lived with his parents, and he was stung by the smoke arising from the sacrifices his daughters-in-law offered to their idols in his own house. Isaac's eyes had suffered earlier in life, too. When he lay bound upon the altar, about to be sacrificed by his father, the angels wept, and their tears fell upon his eyes. There they remained and weakened his sight.

At the same time he had brought blindness upon himself by his love for Esau, since he justified the wicked for a bribe, the bribe of Esau's brotherly love. The loss of vision is the punishment that follows the taking of bribes, as it is said, "A bribe blinds the eyes of the wise" (*Sh'mot* 23:8).

Nevertheless his blindness proved a benefit for Isaac as well as Jacob. In consequence of his physical ailments, Isaac had to stay at home, and so he was spared the pain of being pointed out as the father of the wicked Esau. Also, if his vision had been unimpaired, he would not have blessed Jacob.[xx]

We see here the following reasons for Isaac's blindness:

Punishment for Rebekah's behavior; the result of his being bound on the altar; punishment for his preference of Esau to Jacob; the result of his accepting bribes from Esau; a "gift" of God, to spare Isaac from embarrassment; it was a necessary condition for Jacob to receive his father's blessing.

➢ **What do these six reasons anything in common?**

➢ **Are any of them mutually exclusive?**

➢ **What is the lesson of each one?**

Levi ben Sisi becomes unable to walk

The following Midrash, cited in the Talmud, describes a righteous man's prayer to God for rain. Even the righteous, we discover, can become overly arrogant:

Levi ben Sisi fasted and prayed for rain in vain. He said, 'Master of the world! You have gone up, and taken Your seat in heaven, and show no consideration for (the suffering of) Your children." Rain fell, but Levi became unable to walk. Rav Elazar said, "One must never reproach God."

(*Ta'anit* 25a)

➢ **What was the cause of Levi's inability to walk?**

➢ **Why do the Rabbis repeat this story?**

➢ **What do you think it reflects about their view of one who cannot walk?**

Nahum, Ish Gam-Zo

A striking story is told of an especially saintly man. Nahum Ish Gam-Zo, who suffered terribly.

It was said of Nahum Ish Gam-Zo that he was blind in both eyes, had stump-like hands and legs that were deformed, that his body was covered with boils and that the legs of his bed rested in cups of water so that the ants would not crawl all over him. Once his bed was in an old rickety house. His students wanted to move him and then to remove his possessions. He said to them, "My children, first remove the possessions and then my bed, for be assured, as long as I am in the house it will not collapse." They removed his belongings and then his bed; then the house collapsed. His students asked him, "Our teacher, since you are such a righteous man, how did all of this happen to you?" He said to them, "My children, I brought it upon myself! Once I was walking along the way to my father-in-law's house and I had three loaded mules with me—one with food, one with drinks, and one with gifts. A poor man came up to me on the road and said,

'My friend, feed me.' I said to him, 'Wait until I get down from the mule.' I had not yet finished getting down from the mule when his soul departed. I went and fell upon his face and said, 'My eyes which did not show pity to your eyes, may they be blinded; my hands which did not pity your hands, may they whither; my feet which did not pity your feet, may they become unusable.' Yet my mind was still not eased until I had added, 'May my entire body be covered with boils." They said to him, "Woe is us, that we should see you like this!" He said to them, "Woe is me if you did not see me like this".

(Ta'anit 21a)

Once again we see suffering as a result of punishment with its therapeutic effects brought out. Rav Nahum could not have lived with himself had he not undergone hideous suffering for his supposedly "grave" sin.

The story is most instructive even if much exaggerated. If a righteous man such as Nahum Ish Gam-Zo, upon whom the very walls of the house would not collapse, was punished so severely for such an understandable and human failing, what about most of us who stand on a lower rung of goodness?

> **What is the point of Nahum's response to his students?**

> **According to this Midrash, what is the purpose of his disabilities?**

> **Do you think he wanted them? Do you think he deserved them?**

DISABILITIES AS BLESSING

Since suffering was always seen as an act of God and one could not necessarily find a connection between suffering and a person's actions, other explanation had to be offered. One of these, as illustrated in a story, was that suffering—or, in this instance, having a disability—(as long as it did not effect one's ability to study Torah) was really a blessing, "sufferings of love," which assure one of the future reward:

When sufferings befall you, do you not lose your temper, or reproach God. Rabbi Alexander said, "There is no person to whom no sufferings come: happy is he whose sufferings come to him from the Torah, as it says, 'Teach me from Your Torah." Rabbi Joshua ben Levi said, "All sufferings which befall a person, and prevent him from studying the Torah, are sufferings of reproof; the sufferings which do not prevent him back are sufferings of love."

> **These episodes raise two important issues. First, do you think one can really view a disability as a blessing?**

> **Secondly, the distinction drawn in the Midrash suggests that a serious mental disorder is entirely different from any other type of disability. Do you think it is, and, if so, what makes it qualitatively different from other disabilities?**

Moses' Speech Impairment

Sometimes, it seems that a disability was meant specifically to emphasize the greatness of God, as in the case of Moses' inarticulateness. Even one who has difficulty speaking clearly could, when delivering God's message, become eloquent:

> Moses said furthermore, "I am not an eloquent man, nor can I see of what use words can be in this matter. You are sending me to one who is himself a slave, to Pharaoh of the tribe of Ham, and a slave will not be corrected by words. I consent to go on Your errand only if You give me the power of chastising Pharaoh with brute force." To these words spoken by Moses, God replied, "Do not let it upset you that you are not an eloquent speaker. It is I that made the mouth of all that speak, and I that made men unable to speak. I enable one person to see, another I make blind; one I make to hear, another I make deaf. Had I willed it so, you would have been a man of ready speech. But I desired to show a wonder through you. Whenever I will it, the words I cast into your mouth shall come forth without hesitation. However, what you say about a slave, that he cannot be corrected by words, is true. Therefore I give you My rod for Pharaoh's punishment." [xxi]

In this Midrash, Moses becomes an instrument of God, an embodiment of God's miraculous power. He is unable to speak clearly unless he is delivering God's message, in which case he becomes eloquent.

➢ **How does this midrash offer another way for someone with a disability to view his or hew own disability?**

Bilaam's Blindness

There were times when the enemies of Israel were blinded, as in the case of the people of Sodom who tried to molest the messengers visiting Lot. Also, according to tradition, the non-Israelite prophet Bilaam was blinded as punishment for his attempt to curse the children of Israel:

> Then God said, "Since you speak thus, you shall not curse the people," and added, "O you wicked rascal! I said of Israel, 'Whoever touches them touches the apple of My eye,' and yet you wish to touch them and curse them! Therefore your eye shall be blinded." Thus Bilaam became blind in one eye, as he had already been lame of one foot. [xxii]

➢ **In this passage, God punished an enemy of Israel by making him disabled. How do you view this differently from the previous examples, in which it was someone in the Jewish community who was punished in this way?**

PEOPLE WITH DISABILITIES HEALED IN THE WORLD TO COME

Since it is impossible to say that all of those who suffer find comfort in their lives, another understanding of suffering was proposed. It was suggested that in order to show God's greatness there had to be people who were deaf or blind in this world so that they could be healed in the world to come. Job is pictured in the Midrash as comforting those who come to him suffering from a disability by assuring them that God has not forgotten them:

When anyone with an impairment comes to you, you would console him. To a person who is blind you would say, "If you built yourself a house, you would surely put windows in it, and if God has denied you light, it is so God may be glorified through you in the day when 'the eyes of the blind shall be opened.'" To one who is deaf you would say, "If you fashioned a water pitcher, you would surely not forget to make ears (i.e., handles) for it, and if God created you without hearing, it is so God may be glorified through you in the day when 'the tears of the deaf shall be unstopped.'" In that way you tried to console the weak and the impaired.[xxiii]

A QUESTION OF JUSTICE: IS IT FAIR?

The belief underlying the previous Midrash, that God would heal people with disabilities in the world to come, was an attempt to reconcile reality with the concept of God's justice. Could God, for no apparent reason, randomly afflict certain individuals and not others?

We find this idea expressly stated in the following Midrash:[xxiv]

> Whomever God has smitten in this world is healed in the world to come, for example, those who are blind, unable to walk, and unable to speak, as it says, "Then (in the next world) the eyes of the blind shall be opened, and the ears of the deaf shall be unstopped....." (Isaiah 35:5). As a person goes, so he returns. If he dies blind or deaf or unable to walk, he lives again blind or deaf or unable to walk. Why (is there no change)? If God healed them after they died, the wicked would say "They may not be the same people at all!" "Therefore," says God, "let them arise just as they departed, and only then will I heal them."

There was even the notion that certain righteous individuals could actually affect the nature of God's world by interceding, intentionally or unintentionally, on behalf of people with disabilities. This idea is found in the following Midrash about the birth of Isaac being the cause of miraculous healing:

> The birth of Isaac was a happy event, and not just in the house of Abraham. The whole world rejoiced, for God remembered all barren women at the same time with Sarah; they all bore children. At that time all those who were blind were made to see, all those who could not use their legs were made whole, the ones who were nonverbal were made to speak, and the intellectually impaired were restored to reason.
>
> (*Pesikta Rabbati* 42, on *Bereshit* 21:1)

There is also a beautiful Midrash about the midwives, Shifrah and Puah, who saved the infant males by disobeying Pharaoh's decree to kill them at birth:

> They made supplication to God, praying, "You know that we are not fulfilling the words of Pharaoh, but it is our aim to fulfill Your words. O may it be Your will, our Lord, to let the child come into the world healthy, so we are not suspected of trying of slay it, maiming it in the attempt." The Lord listened to their prayer, and no child born under the care of Shifrah and Puah (or Yocheved and Miriam, as the midwives are also called), came into the world unable to use their legs or blind or afflicted with any other blemish.
>
> (*Sh'mot Rabbah* 1:15)

The implications of these sources may be troubling to some of us. How are we to accept the idea that had Isaac not been born or had the midwives not prayed to God, children would have been born with disabilities? How are we to deal with the notion that whether or not someone is cured depends upon who is praying for him or her? These are important questions which will continue to motivate a variety of responses. The Rabbis often felt that since disabilities were seen as an evil in life, and since God was the cause of all, people with disabilities were less worthy, somehow tainted or inferior. Therefore, accepting the idea of God's ultimate control over all human events made many of the *midrashic* explanations quite comforting.

BLINDNESS AS DEATH?

Four types of people, the Midrash claims, were accounted as dead:

> ..... the poor, someone with leprosy (or a particular skin ailment), someone who is blind, and one who has no children.
>
> (*Nedarim* 64b)

Pity

Often those with disabilities were pitied and looked upon as "unfortunates":

> "…..Who fed you in the wilderness with manna... in order to try you with hardships" (Deuteronomy 9:16). R. Ami and R. Assi (had different interpretations). One said, "One who has food in his basket is not like one who does not have food in his basket" (since he eats and worries about tomorrow's meal). The other said, "One who sees and eats is not like one who does not see and eats." R. Yosef (who was blind) said, "Here there is a reference to the blind, who eat and are never satisfied." Abaye said, "Therefore, one who eats a meal should only eat it in the daytime" (so it can be seen)!
>
> (*Yoma* 74b)

This can be categorized as "folk-wisdom" which reflects the view that the blind are "unfortunate," since they cannot fully enjoy life. In this way someone who is blind could have been considered as partially "dead" (in that his or her eyes do not function).

> ➢ **Are there other conditions which might be considered partial "death"?**

> ➢ **How might one interpret the blessing in the Amidah which calls God *m'hayei hameitim*, "who restores the 'dead' to life"?**

IN THE WILDERNESS

There is a Midrash which suggests that during the *Sh'mot* from Egypt many Israelites had disabilities. The Midrash says that God did not feel it appropriate to give the Torah to such "imperfect" beings, so God waited a short time, healed them all, and then gave them the Torah:

> R. Joshua ben Levi said, "When Israel went out of Egypt there were among them those who were blemished from the hard labor. Since they worked with clay and bricks, a stone would fall upon someone from a building breaking his arm or deforming his leg. The Holy One said, "It is not fitting that I should give my Torah to those with blemishes."

What did he do? He hinted to the heavenly angels, and they went down and healed the people.

CAN SOMEONE BLIND BE TRUSTED?

There were Rabbis who considered a person who is blind unreliable to transmit the words of tradition, which was supposed to be done precisely and accurately.

> "Most people will proclaim each one his own goodness" (Proverbs 20:6—this refers to everyone else. "But who can find a faithful person?" (ibid.)—this refers to R. Zayra, who said, "We do not have to concern ourselves with the transmissions of R. Sheshet, since he is blind."[xxv]

Evidently, Rabbi Zayra felt that since Rav Sheshet could not actually see who was doing the talking he could not be relied upon to report accurately with the correct name of the speaker. Therefore, he was not to be trusted.

CAN PEOPLE WHO ARE BLIND OWN CARS?

from "Five Reasons Why People Who are Blind Should Own Their Own Cars" By Danny Siegel[xxvi]

First, we have to begin with microwave ovens for blind people. Blind people might benefit from having microwave ovens because:

1. They are safer.
2. They go "bing" when the cooking or defrosting or reheating is finished and the popcorn or soup or casserole or baked apple is ready.
3. Everyone else has microwave ovens.
4. Many new microwaveable foods are coming out which allow for a wider range of nutritional benefits.
5. *Everyone* has microwave ovens.
6. It is easy to put Braille on the keyboard.
7. You don't have to plan so far ahead, and why should blind people — just because they cannot see — have to plan their meals differently than people who can see?
8. There are probably 15 other good reasons why, which anyone can figure out if he or she just sits down and thinks about it or sits down with a friend and talks about it.

Now, to the cars. Here are some reasons why blind people might want to own cars:

1. Everyone else has one.
2. They might need to go somewhere, and a friend or neighbor who usually drives them to that somewhere might have his or her own car tied up at that moment, and if the person who is blind didn't have a car, he or she couldn't get to the right place at the right time. The most common example would be the friend's teen-age kid took the car out for a date or a night with friends down at the bowling alley, ice cream shop, or miniature golf course. This is by no means uncommon.
3. In case of emergency, there *has to be* an available car. It is life-saving, an issue of *Pikuach Nefesh*.
4. The blind car owner can lend the car out to someone else who needs it, just like everyone else does in similar situations. The right to lend is a matter of human dignity. The only difference is that one car owner can see and the other cannot.
5. One of the people in the audience once mentioned that this is a matter of personal property protection: when someone goes away on a week's vacation, he or she cancels the news-paper or asks the neighbors to take it off the lawn so a potential burglar won't come by and take out the TV, VCR, computer, and jewelry. If some disreputable persons cruise the neighborhood looking for a likely candidate for a break-in, if they see a car in the driveway of every house except for the one where the person who is blind lives, it makes the person who is blind a more likely victim.

Solved by:

John Fling, Mitzvah hero, Columbia, SC.[xxvii] He bought a car for his blind friend, Emily McKinsey (she could not afford one for herself), so she could do errands, go to the store, the movies, a picnic, anywhere she needed to go, without having to ask the neighbors to drive her around in *their* cars.

EUPHEMISM: L'SHON SAGI-NAHOR

The Midrash reflects great compassion and sensitivity for people with disabilities. Some of this can be seen in the terminology which the Rabbis used. Instead of calling someone who was blind a *suma,* they would often use the term *sagi nahor* (literally, "full of light") or *me'or aynayim* (literally, "enlightened eyes"). These are not sarcastic terms, but a true reflection of the rabbinic attitude, as we shall see.

There are two beautiful Midrashim about sensitivity to the blind shown by Rav Eliezer and Rav Hoshiah:

> R. Eliezer ben Yacov invited a man who is blind to dinner, and he placed him in a position at the table even more honored that his own. The others said, "This must be a great man, or R. Eliezer would not have placed him above himself at the table." Therefore, they showed him much respect. "To what do I owe this?" the man asked them. They replied, "Because R. Eliezer placed you above himself at the table." Then the man prayed for him as follows: "You have shown loving kindness to him who is seen, but cannot see, May God who sees but cannot be seen, receive your graciousness, and show loving-kindness to you."
>
> (*Yerushalmi Pe'ah* 8:9)

R. Hoshiah employed a man who was blind as a teacher for his son, and he used to dine with R. Hoshiah. One day R Hoshiah had guests, and he did not invite the man to eat with him. In the evening he (R. Hoshiah) went to him and said, "Let my master not be annoyed with me; I had guests, and I did not want you to be held in low esteem, and not receive due honor. That is why I did not have you eat with me today." The man said, "You have appeased him who is seen and doesn't see; may God who sees and is unseen receive your appeasement."

(*Yerushalmi Pe'ah* 8:9)

These two stories were meant to serve as an example for everyone who came in contact with someone who was disabled. Blindness was seen as simply an external condition, not in any way affecting the worth of the individual or the respect due to him.

THE GIFTED ONES

In fact, people with disabilities were actually seen at times as people with very special gifts and contributions to make. Look at the following Midrash about Mordecai and someone who was deaf:

(Another) one of Mordecai's epithets was Bilshan, "master of languages." Being a member of the great Sanhedrin he understood all the seventy languages spoken in the world. More than that, he knew the language of those who were deaf and nonverbal. It once happened that no new grain could be obtained at Passover time. A person who was deaf and nonverbal came and pointed with one hand to the roof and with the other to the cottage. Mordecai understood that these signs meant a locality by the name of *Gagot-Ts'rifim* (literally, "Cottage-Roofs"), and, lo, new grain was found there for the Omer offering. On another occasion a person who was both deaf and nonverbal pointed with one hand to his eye and with the other to the staple of the bolt on the door. Mordecai understood that he meant a place called *Ein-Soker* ("dry well") since eye and spring are same word (*ein*) in Aramaic, and *sikra* also has a two meanings, staple and exhaustion.

(Based on Ginzberg, Legends, vol. 6, 382-83)

This Midrash is especially instructive in that it points to the difficulty of communication. The Rabbis realized that a large part of our attitudes toward people with disabilities was the result of prejudice and ignorance—due to our inability to communicate adequately.

In the following story about a man who is blind, you will see that what he lacked in his sense of sight was more than compensated for by his "insight," as he confronted prejudice and ignorance:

Rav Sheshet was blind. Once all the people went out to see the King, and R. Sheshet arose and went with them. A certain Sadducean (a member of a sect which disagreed with many principles of the dominant group of *Talmudic* Rabbis, the Pharisees) came across him and said to him, "The whole pitchers go to the river, but where do the broken ones go?" He replied, "I will show you that I know more than you." The first troop of soldiers passed by and a shout arose. The Sadducean said, "The king is coming."

R. Sheshet replied, "The king is not coming." A second troop passed by and there was silence. R. Sheshet said, "Now indeed the king is coming." The

Sadducean said him, "How did you know this?" He replied "Because the earthly royalty is like the heavenly. And it is written, 'Go forth and stand upon the mount before the Lord. And behold, the Lord passed by and a great and strong wind rent the mountains, and broke the rocks in pieces before the Lord; but the Lord was not in the wind; and after the wind an earthquake; but the Lord was not in the earthquake; and after the earthquake a fire; but the Lord was not in the fire; and after the fire a still small voice (I Kings 19:11-12)." When the king came, R Sheshet said the blessing over him (the blessing for seeing a king). The Sadducean said to him, "You, you say a blessing for one whom you do not see?" What happened to that Sadducean? Some say that his companions put his eyes out; others say that R Sheshet cast his eyes upon him and he became a heap of bones.

(*B'rachot* 58a)

Perhaps his gives us a better understanding of why a person who is blind was called "full of light" or "enlightened eyes"!

CONCLUSION

The Midrash or Aggadah reflects well the rabbinic attitude toward people with disabilities, and we have seen that it is certainly not monolithic. There are a few points to make in summary:

- It was felt that there was some connection between a person's disabilities and his or her actions.
- There was also a belief that disabilities were part of God's overall plan and that which was "crooked" in this world would be "cured" in the next.
- We find a deep belief in the ultimate justice of God which at times was beyond the understanding or even the life-span of a human being.
- The Rabbis believed that those who had disabilities were extremely unfortunate and were to be pitied for their suffering.
- Above all, the Midrash calls for compassion and understanding—to be sensitive to the needs and feelings of people with disabilities and to recognize their value as human beings beyond their disability.

Now that we have looked at the *halahic* and midrashic sources to understand the rabbinic attitudes towards people with disabilities, we turn now to ask, "Who Makes People Unique?"

Chapter Six—Who Makes People Unique

THEOLOGICAL IMPLICATIONS

In this final section of our study, the emphasis of the title has been changed, for here we ask the question: Who makes people unique and why?

What is God's Image?

God's image is not a physical thing. All physical things are limited to time and space and God, being unlimited, cannot be physical.

God's image is a unique capacity/ capability/ sense that no other living creature has self-awareness: we are like God in that we know we exist and have an understanding of all the consequences of self-awareness—to act freely, to understand a moral code, with aptitude to act rationally:

וַיִּבְרָא אֱלֹהִים | אֶת־הָאָדָם בְּצַלְמוֹ בְּצֶלֶם
אֱלֹהִים בָּרָא אֹתוֹ זָכָר וּנְקֵבָה בָּרָא אֹתָם :

God created the Human in God's own image…
male and female, God created them….
(*Bereishit* 1:27)

➤ **What does it mean to be created in the image of God?**

➤ **Is it pretentious or boastful of us to think that we are created in the divine image?**

➤ **What challenges might this bring?**

➤ **What do you think makes people unique?**

➤ **How does the concept of *B'tzelem Elohim* affect the idea of uniqueness?**

Consider this text again that was found in the introduction to this book:

> If a person strikes several coins from the same die, they all resemble one another. But, although God fashioned every man in the stamp of the first man [Adam], not a single one is exactly like his fellow. (*Sanhedrin* 4:5)

➤ **How do you explain our differences if we were all created in God's image?**

➤ **What might be some of the things that were created in God's image if we all look and act differently?**

➤ **Do you think that having a disability is a blessing?**

A disability may indeed be a blessing, but is one in disguise. For a person with a disability, it is the way they are—some people have blond hair, some people have brown. Some people can use their legs, and some can not. Some people can see and some can not. All are made in the image of God and disabilities are accepted as a natural part of life. We do not wish a severe disability upon someone, but nor can we say that they have been created as any less of a person who is *B'tzelem Elohim*. A disability is not a curse and it may even be, as we will see in the following chapter, an impetus to positive action and new possibilities. One would not wish for a disability; one can live with it and make the best of it, but, all things considered, it would probably be better if no one had a disability. Nonetheless, we do bless them and thank God that people are created differently.

Why then do some people become disabled and some not? Why are some people born with a disability and some with none?

We have seen some of the Midrashic attempts answer these questions. The Midrash suggested these responses, among others:

Physical disabilities are signs of punishment.
Suffering can be beneficial.
Disabilities in this world will be healed in the next.
Suffering is necessary to show the greatness of God.
We don't always understand the way world works.

RESPONSES TO SUFFERING

If we agree, however, that having a disability makes life more challenging, then we must account for its presence. Typical of Jewish thinking, there is not one response offered to cover all situations. Milton Steinberg in his classic book Basic Judaism categorizes some of the more traditional Jewish responses. They can be summarized in the following way:

Moral responses

The most traditional understanding of suffering accounts for it in several ways as part of a moral/ethical value system:

- Suffering can be punishment for a sin which was committed by an individual, although the person may not even be aware of having committed that sin. The sin may be ritualistic or ethical in nature.

- Since every individual is part of a larger whole, one's suffering could be the result of the sins or failing of the community. One who lives in a community casts his or her lot with it and is responsible for the conduct of that community.

- Suffering is a means of strengthening the individual. It is, in a way, an adversary against whom to struggle and grow stronger. Our suffering builds character and a strong will. As has been said often, a Jew is like an egg: the more you cook it, the harder it gets.

Metaphysical responses

- Perhaps what we regard as suffering is not really that. However, since we can see only a partial view of the whole picture, we are unable to understand it. There may be a purpose which is hidden from us, but which ultimately serves our interests or the larger good.

- What we call suffering may simply be the result of the natural laws striking us adversely. If we are prepared to accept the benefits of these natural laws, what right do we have to complain when they work to our disadvantage?

The World to Come

- There are those who explain that suffering in this world will be compensated in the hereafter. This would account for the cases when it seems that the righteous suffer and the wicked are thriving. Also those with disabilities will be healed in the world to come.

- In fact, the fundamental imperfections of the human race are mirrored in the imperfections of the individual. Nothing in this world is perfect and it will not be until the end of days, when God's plan is completely worked out, that the world and all human beings will be perfected.

The Mystery

Finally, there is the theory that all suffering is a mystery, one which we humans could not hope ever to understand fully. Only God in His infinite wisdom knows every cause and every reason, and it is a mark of humility to accept this fact.

IS IT ADEQUATE?

Perhaps for traditionalists, some of these responses have been comforting and have enabled them to accept, if not fully understand, their suffering or the suffering of their loved ones. It must be noted, however, that all of the above explanations involved God as either the active causer of suffering, or at least a willing and purposeful agent, allowing it to exist.

While this approach leaves one's basic faith intact, this is an age when very challenging questions are being asked. In the post-Holocaust years when the connection between a person's deeds and his suffering cannot be conscious, a new understanding is sought.

WHEN BAD THINGS HAPPEN

Harold Kushner offers another understanding of God's role in our lives and the meaning of suffering. His idea is applicable to our discussion:[xxviii]

> All the responses to tragedy which we have considered have a least one thing in common. They all assume that God is the cause of our suffering, and they try to understand why God would want us to suffer. Is it for own good, or is it a punishment we deserve, or could it be that God does not care what happens to us? Many of the answers were sensitive and imaginative, but none was totally satisfying. Some led us to blame ourselves in order to spare God's reputation. Others asked us to deny reality or to repress our true feelings. We were left either hating ourselves for deserving such a fate, or hating God for sending it to us when we did not deserve it.

There may be another approach. Maybe God does not cause our suffering. Maybe it happens for some reason other than the will of God. The psalmist writes, "I lift mine eyes to the hills; from where does my help come? My help comes from the Lord, maker of Heaven and earth." (Psalm 121:1-2). He does not say, "My pain comes from the Lord," or "my tragedy comes from the Lord." He says "my help comes from the Lord."

Could it be that God does not cause the bad things that happen to us? Could it be that God doesn't decide which families shall give birth to a child with disabilities, that God did not single out Ron to be paralyzed by a bullet or Helen to have a degenerative disease, but rather that God stands ready to help them and us cope with our tragedies if we could only get beyond the feelings of guilt and anger that separate us from God? Could it be that "How could God do this to me?" is really the wrong question to ask?

Perhaps there is nothing to understand and that it is best that we realize this. For once we can see God's role as "helper" and "sustainer," then we can begin to derive strength from God in our suffering. Then we can realize that our role is to help others who suffer, just as God helps them, and that God helps them through us.

Adopting this view also relieves us of the burden of justifying God and makes it clear to us that being disabled is not a stigma any more than is being born with blue eyes.

People just are different, and this is the beauty of our world. Many coins have been stamped from the same mold, yet no two are alike. "Blessed are You, Lord our God, King of the Universe, who makes people different!"

JACOB WHO LOVES THE SABBATH[xxix]
By Rabbi Bradley Shavit Artson

God has shown you, O mortal, what is good: to walk humbly with your God. (Micah 6:8)

For ten years, I served as a congregational rabbi in the suburbs of Orange County, California, delivering many passionate sermons on the holiness of the Sabbath. I spoke of the need to reserve one day each week devoted to contemplation, to community, and to God. Quoting sources ancient and modern, I urged my congregants to abandon the headlong pursuit of elusive chores, of work never completed, and instead, on this one day, to savor the simple wonder of being. But despite all those years of preaching Shabbat, and even though I myself was Sabbath-observant, I don't think I truly understood my own message or felt the full power of the seventh day until after I left the congregation. It was only after my family moved to the city that my six-year old son Jacob showed me how to engage in the true soul-rest of the Sabbath.

Jacob gave me the gift of the Sabbath.

Jacob is autistic. His mind perceives the world in ways different from most people; his sense of timing and priorities follows its own inner schedule. The agendas that consume most of us simply don't exist for him. Jacob is indifferent to matters of social status. He loves what he loves, and he loves whom he loves. Jacob is passionate about his family, for example, cuddling in our bed early in the morning, sitting side-by-side as we read together, laughing as we chase one another in the park. And Jacob is passionate about the Torah, transforming a stray stick into a Torah scroll; he cradles the branch in his arms while he chants the synagogue melodies. Marching his "Torah" around the room, Jacob sings the ancient Psalms of David with same joyous intensity of the ancient singer of Israel. One of the insights - and challenges - of his autism is that unless Jacob loves it, it doesn't get his attention.

Now freed from my obligation to arrive at services early, to stand on the pulpit, and to lead the congregation in prayer once we moved to the city, I looked forward to savoring the early Shabbat morning walk to our new synagogue with my son. On our first Sabbath there, I tried to walk the way most other people walk. I wanted to arrive punctually. Jacob, on the other hand, was already where he wanted to be: enjoying a walk with his Abba. I cajoled, pulled, pushed, yelled, but Jacob would not rush. I told him we were going to miss services, and still he strolled. I insisted that he hurry, and he paused to explore a patch of flowers, or sat himself down in the warm morning sun. I tried grabbing his hand and pulling him by force. I tried walking behind him and pushing with my knees. Nothing worked. By the time we arrived at the synagogue, hopelessly late, my stomach was in knots. I was drenched in sweat, and far too frustrated to pray.

You Can Fly: Letting A Boy With Autism Speak for Himself

Selected Writings of Jacob Artson

Before I learned to type I was invisible and lonely because I couldn't speak, so I was isolated and couldn't participate. When I was almost 7 years old, my Ema and I met an amazing speech therapist who introduced us to facilitated communication. My Ema provides support and resistance to my arm so I can focus and keep my thoughts and body movements organized while I say what I want.

I always have something to say and now I can finally say it. I know I am not the only nonverbal autistic boy in the world who can be part of the world thanks to facilitated communication, so please contact my Ema and she'll help you get started on a journey of discovery!

Jacob Artson, age 12

The second week repeated the aggravation of the first. We still reached services late, and I was so annoyed that I couldn't even sit still when we did get to the sanctuary.

This last week, I realized that something had to give. Jacob wasn't going to stop being Jacob, which meant that our walk would have to proceed his way, on his schedule. Resigned to slow frustration, I decided to make the best of it; I would learn to walk the way Jacob walked, but I would take a book. I chose as companion a medieval mystical text, the *Tomer Devorah, The Palm Tree of Deborah*, a meditation on Kabbalah and ethics by Rabbi Moshe Cordovero. Book in hand, I abandoned any commitment to schedule or pace.

As Jacob and I and Rabbi Cordovero set out on walk number three, I tried paying no attention to our speed or direction. When I got to the corner, I didn't let myself look at the light - invariably green until right before Jacob caught up. Instead, I read.

It's impossible to read quickly while walking, to focus on how many pages are already finished. Reading while walking is a form of meditation: savoring individual words, you find yourself delighting in phrases. To the prophet Micah's praise, "Who is like You, God?" Rabbi Cordovero responds "*there is no moment that people are not nourished and sustained by the Divine power bestowed upon them. Thus no persons ever sin against God without God, at that very moment, bestowing abundant vitality upon them. Even though they may use this very vitality to transgress, God is not withholding. Instead the Bountiful One suffers the insult and continues to enable the limbs to move.*" The words on the page melded with my walk: I could feel life's vitality infusing my own, making this very walk a celebration. The sunshine streamed into my soul, God bestowing life and love without conditions or restraint.

As I walked and read, the stroll was punctuated by the intense fragrance of a colorful bouquet. The words of the *Tomer Devorah* reframed the morning song of a bird into an outpouring of creation's gratitude to God. The egglike flowers of the dogwood trees seemed to gesture the words of the psalmist, "*How manifold are your works, O Lord. In wisdom have you made them all.*" In the towering palm trees we passed, I could feel the call of the prophet Isaiah, "*Before you, mount and hill shall shout aloud, and all the trees of the field shall clap their hands.*"

From time to time, I just turned to relish my son's meandering. His joy was contagious: the pure delight of a little boy with his Abba and with time. And his joy was pure. My son cannot read, yet his very presence, I could now see, affirmed the words of Kohelet that "*there is nothing better than for one to rejoice in what he is doing.*" Occasionally, I found myself slipping into my old apprehensions, worrying about what part of the service I was missing, or fretting about not proceeding quickly enough. But the allure of my book, the walk, the sun, and my son, restored me. Jacob's spirit had become infectious.

When we finally did arrive at the synagogue, the service was more than halfway over. They were already putting the Torah scroll back into the Ark. Jacob squealed with delight, "The Torah! The Torah!" and ran to the front of the sanctuary. Too excited to stand still, he bounced on his toes next to the person holding the Scroll, while the congregation recited the ancient praise: "*Hodo al eretz v'shamayim!* God's glory encompasses heaven and earth!" My spirit soared, for I had just borne witness to that glory in the flowers ablaze in color and light, in the delicate breeze swirling through the leaves. "God exalts and extols the faithful, the people Israel, who are close to God. *Halleluyah!*"

More than any sermon I've ever heard or given, I owe the fullness of the Shabbat to my son.

Jacob taught me through his own example that we can't possibly be late, because, wherever we are, we are already where we are supposed to be. Our minds just have to acknowledge what our heart already knows. Jacob has taught me how to walk with God.

I learned that day that Shabbat is the cultivated art of letting go, letting be, and letting in. In that art, Jacob is my teacher, my master, my Rebbe.

SELECTED WRITINGS OF JACOB ARTSON

Hillel
May 10, 2004

Hillel was a great teacher of Torah. I love Hillel's saying that you should never judge a person until you are in his or her shoes. I have often felt judged by people who look at me and think I am retarded because I can't speak or move the way most people can. Hillel probably didn't know anyone who had autism but his teachings are very meaningful to me because I love Torah just as he did, and it is very comforting to know that great Jews like Hillel have taught about me without even knowing me. I learn from him that I also need to be more patient with people and try to see their perspective before I make negative judgments about them.

The Torah helps me keep my hope and helps me keep working hard to be like other kids. I am very grateful to all of you for supporting my Hebrew School class so I can learn about how to be a good Jew and a person who earns respect.

Hillel is a wonderful role model for all people whether they have special needs or not. I have learned from Hillel that I can be a role model by living his teachings and that I am responsible for my behavior just like all typically developing people are responsible for the way they treat other people. I am very happy that I was born Jewish because this is a terrific way to live in the world as a partner with God and all of God's creation.

Part of Your World
March 14, 2005

My favorite song is "Part of Your World." In it, Ariel is conflicted over whether to stay in her mermaid world or leave for the human world. Even though Sebastian tries to persuade her that not everything in the human world is positive, she only sees the negative aspects of her world and the positive side of the human world. She ends up leaving her family forever in order to marry the man she loves. I am glad they made a sequel so that Ariel's daughter could bring their family back together. I think Ariel made the wrong choice because I would never leave my family for a princess. Often I am sad to be autistic, but the neurotypical world is far from perfect, and I am blessed with many family and friends who combine the best of both.

Chapter Seven—What can we do?

אַל תִּפְרוֹשׁ מִן הַצִּבּוּר
"DO NOT SEPARATE YOURSELF FROM THE COMMUNITY"
Pirke Avot 2:4

> **What is a community? What does it mean to not separate from it?**

> **What are my responsibilities?**

> **What can we do? What should we do, based upon what we've learned about our responsibility as a community?**

WHAT IS YOUR ATTITUDE?

What is your attitude towards people with disabilities? Is there a difference between "caring" and "patronizing"? Do we make someone more uncomfortable and self-conscious is we pointedly try to ignore what is right in front of us?

In dealing with our own attitudes, we might want to ask some of these questions:

- ☐ How do I feel when I am in the presence of someone who has a disability?
- ☐ Do I have any friends who have a disability? If not, are there any particular reasons?
- ☐ When I see someone who has a disability, do I look at the person or at the disability?
- ☐ Do I talk differently to someone with a disability?
- ☐ Do I avoid eye contact when talking with people with disabilities?
- ☐ Do I speak for people with a speech or language disability when they are capable of answering for themselves?
- ☐ Do I avoid touching a person with a disability?
- ☐ Do I hear myself saying, "She can't do that because she is disabled," before I have met the person?
- ☐ Do I avoid asking people with disabilities a question because I am afraid it will upset them?
- ☐ Do I feel sorry for people with disabilities?
- ☐ Do I find myself thinking of the disability before I think of the person?
- ☐ Do I find myself speaking of people with disabilities as a group? Example: "Blind people are good in music."

A Self Analysis

True or False

1. Using a wheelchair means the end of a fulfilling life.
   ☐ True ☐ False

2. Slow speech is a sign of a slowed mental process.
   ☐ True ☐ False

3. Having a vision disability means you are unable to give directions.
   ☐ True ☐ False

4. People with disabilities are usually in need of, or want, assistance.
   ☐ True ☐ False

5. Most people who are deaf read lips.
   ☐ True ☐ False

6. Being blind means a person lives in total darkness.
   ☐ True ☐ False

7. Hearing impaired and hard-of-hearing are the same thing.
   ☐ True ☐ False

8. Having a mobility disability does not mean that you have other disabilities.
   ☐ True ☐ False

9. A person who is deaf can have excellent speech.
   ☐ True ☐ False

10. Most people who are deaf cannot make sound with their voice.
    ☐ True ☐ False

11. Having a vision disability gives someone super-hearing, super-touch or super-smell.
    ☐ True ☐ False

12. Having slow speech does not mean you can't or don't want to talk for yourself.
    ☐ True ☐ False

13. Finger spelling is a form of Sign Language.
    ☐ True ☐ False

14. People paralyzed from the waist down cannot have children.
    ☐ True ☐ False

15. People with communication disabilities may be mistaken for a person who is drunk.
    ☐ True ☐ False

You see a person with a severe limp approaching the door, and you rush to open it for her. She responds by saying, "Oh that's okay. I can do it myself."

 ➢ **How do you feel and how do you react?**

 ➢ **What do you want to do? What do you feel is an appropriate response?**

 ➢ **Are your views toward the disabled reflected in your actions?**

Perhaps the greatest handicapper of all is society's attitude toward people with disabilities. This problem has only recently begun to be recognized and taken seriously. We have come a long way in making many of our institutions more accessible to individuals with disabilities, although much more work and thought are still required:[xxx]

> For the most part, however, people still view individuals with disabilities as lesser people—to be pitted, feared or ignored. These attitudes may arise from fear of someone who is different in any way or simply from a lack of knowledge about disabilities. Despite good intentions and education programs, negative stereotypes and callous behavior remain.

This (chapter) gives suggestions on how to relate to people with disabilities, how to look beyond the disability and look at the ability and the personality—the things that make each of us unique and worthwhile.

EXERCISE

ROLE PLAY
Below, are a few scenarios. After reading the scenario, go back and re-read it and change one of the characters to be someone with a disability. How does your impression change?

Situation 1: You notice Kim sitting in the corner during opening dance. You go up to her and try to get her to join. She refuses. What is your impression of Kim? Does your impression change if you knew that Kim was diagnosed with autism?

Situation 2: You are working in a fast food restaurant. Brian, the French-fryer, slams down the basked in frustration. He yells, "I don't understand the directions. I'm so stupid!" and starts to walk away. What is your impression of Brian? Does your impression change if you knew that Brian was diagnosed with a learning disability? How can you be a source of support and encouragement to him?

Situation 3: Danny, who has Down's Syndrome, is a very friendly person. He loves to hug people—especially you, as you have discovered. How do you feel when he constantly hugs you and what do you do about it?

Situation 4: Jason likes to sing to himself in public, out loud. He tends to do this at inappropriate times (like at the beginning of services or in a movie). You feel embarrassed by him. How do you mend the situation without hurting him or embarrassing yourself?

ATTITUDES AND BARRIERS

A person with a disability is—first and foremost—a person. While a particular disability may limit certain types of activities or abilities, it does not make the individual any less a person. Ten to 15 percent of the population has a disability such as blindness, deafness, paralysis, cerebral palsy, neurological disorder, mental illness, arthritis or an intellectual impairment.

An attitude is a feeling or emotion which a person has towards a fact, situation or person. Awareness is the knowledge or perception about a situation, object or person. Attitudinal barriers are a way of thinking or feeling that blocks or limits people's perception of the potential of disabled people to be capable, independent individuals. Attitudinal barriers include prejudice, ignorance, fear insensitivity, bigotry, stereotyping, misconception, discrimination, dislike, insecurity, discomfort, tension and intolerance.

Positive attitudes and awareness help people who do not have disabilities in their contacts and relationships with people who have disabilities. Attitudes which are insensitive and prejudicial produce poor relationships. A person may not be aware of biases or negative attitudes and may express them in words or actions.

You Can Fly
By Jacob Artson
April 17, 2005

If you look long and hard
Maybe you'll see why
Everyone has a talent
And they can learn to fly

If you look long and hard
You can see beyond the face
It doesn't speak but it still feels
That everyone has a place

If you look long and hard
There's a secret you will learn
That love is something we all
can share
And no one has to earn

If you look long and hard
At any girl or guy
Maybe you can be the one
To show them how to fly!

Devices Will Help Deaf Israelis 'Hear' War Alerts
Excerpted from: Cybercast News Service - 14 Feb 2003
By Julie Stahl, CNSNews.com Jerusalem Bureau Chief

Jerusalem (CNSNews.com) - North American Jewish communities raised more than $1 million to purchase thousands of special devices that will help hearing impaired people in Israel "hear" warning sirens and receive civil defense instructions from the Home Front Command in the event of an Iraqi missile attack on Israel.

During the last Gulf War in 1991, Israelis were warned to don their gas masks and enter their sealed rooms by sirens and radio messages, but that created a problem for the hearing impaired.

It was a "serious issue" for these people that they could not hear warning sirens or listen to information about when to leave their sealed rooms or take off their gas masks at the end of an alert, said Jeff Kaye, of the Jewish Agency's Israel Emergency Campaign (IEC).
There were stories of deaf people living in Ramat Gan (where many missiles hit in 1991) who were in buildings where missiles came down and others whose neighbors went to their doors and banged and banged, trying to alert them to an impending attack, Kaye said.

But this time if Israel is attacked things will be different.

Distributed by the Home Front Command and the Association of the Deaf in Israel, 7,059 hearing impaired Israelis have received beepers, which will enable them to "hear" announcements like everyone else.

The beepers are connected directly to the Home Front Command Headquarters and will inform the hearing impaired immediately of an impending attack or other relevant instructions.

The devices vibrate and have flashing lights and bells that alert the user that there is an incoming text message on the beeper. They are available in several different languages and were distributed regardless of race, religion or length of stay in Israel.

ATTITUDES IN THE JEWISH WORLD

Obviously people who have disabilities encounter similar difficulties, regardless of their religions. However, since we are studying Jewish attitudes in particular, let's look at the story of one Jew with a disability and his reflections:

> I was a "blue baby." At birth, the supply of oxygen to my brain was interrupted. This left me with a condition known as cerebral palsy. If you were to meet me on the street you would notice that I am "different." My speech is slurred; my walk is awkward; I have limited use of my hands. But, I can do almost everything that I have to for myself. I do not use canes or crutches to assist me in walking, and daily living skills, such as dressing, feeding, and bathing myself, also do not pose a problem.
>
> > The hardest obstacles I have been forced to cope with over the years were not my own physical limitations, but the attitude of other people. For instance, when I was six my parents tried to enroll me in an afternoon Talmud Torah. The

administrators of the school refused to accept me because they felt that I did not have the intellectual capacity to successfully take part in the program. (Since then I have earned degrees at both the graduate and undergraduate levels and I was accepted as a student in the Graduate School of Journalism at Columbia.)[xxxi]

This account is a painful one. The author, Martin Kroessel, goes on to relate his view that the attitude of the Jewish community is actually less enlightened than what he found elsewhere. Whether or not that can be documented and even without comparing the reactions of different religious groups, it is worthwhile for us to look at our own community. It is a fallacy to believe that because we do not see many Jews who are disabled in synagogues, there are proportionally fewer Jews with disabilities than in the general population. The proper question to ask is: why don't we see them in synagogues?

EXERCISE

Why don't you think we see more Jewish people with disabilities in our synagogues? What do you think may be keeping them from being a part of the Jewish community? Name some obstacles (including obstacles other than physical obstacles) in your synagogue and suggest ways of removing them:

OBSTACLE	REMEDY/ SOLUTION

Go back to the above list and add the consequence that inaction would bring:

OBSTACLE	CONSEQUENCE

Kroessel suggests the following reason:

Most of the people with disabilities I know can be described, at best, as being indifferent to their Judaism. And who can blame them? Throughout the life of a person with a disability, barriers are encountered to active participation in Jewish life. For instance, it is well-understood that Jewish education plays a critical role in first exposing children to their religious and cultural pupils with disabilities. Indeed, until very recently special education was virtually nonexistent within

Jewish education. Most synagogues and other communal institutions were equally as ill-prepared to deal with people with disabilities. It is a tragic irony that while lay and religious leaders profess to be concerned about assimilation, the Jewish community remains content with a situation that makes is impossible for a large number of persons with disabilities to be affiliated with communal institutions.[xxxii]

This brings us to another important issue, one that is relevant and that should demand our attention.

Reflect about attitudes evident in the congregation toward people with disabilities, and use this list as a springboard for discussion:

☐ Are persons with disabilities welcome to pray with us? If not, what are we doing wrong?

☐ Are there members with not apparent disabilities?

☐ Do we recognize the gifts of people with disabilities and are they fully involved in the life of the congregation?

☐ Are people with disabilities given opportunities to serve others within the congregation and in the outreach programs?

☐ Are positions of leadership offered to individuals who happen to have disability?

☐ How does the congregation respond to religious or lay leader, who acquire a serious disability?

CREATING ACCESS: CREATING A BARRIER FREE HOUSE OF WORSHIP

Many people with disabilities have had negative experiences in synagogues, simply because they can't get in. Often it is just thoughtlessness and oftentimes it is things that are easy to overcome.

When buildings are structurally inaccessible, those with mobility impairments cannot get in. When the prayers are only spoken, those with hearing problems are denied some or all of the messages. When announcements are in print form only, those with poor sight miss opportunities. When general invitations are issued and members with a mental illness or another chronic illness are not personally invited, they may assume they are excluded. When leadership appointments are made and each person selected appears to be physically or mentally "perfect," the person with a disability may doubt his or her own usefulness. [xxxiii]

"A lot of people think access means the ability to get into a building, no matter where or how you can get into it, whether you get into it through a back alley, or through an elevator that usually carries garbage or food. But shouldn't it mean that you can get into the building through the front door with everybody else?"

Itzhak Perlman, The New York Times

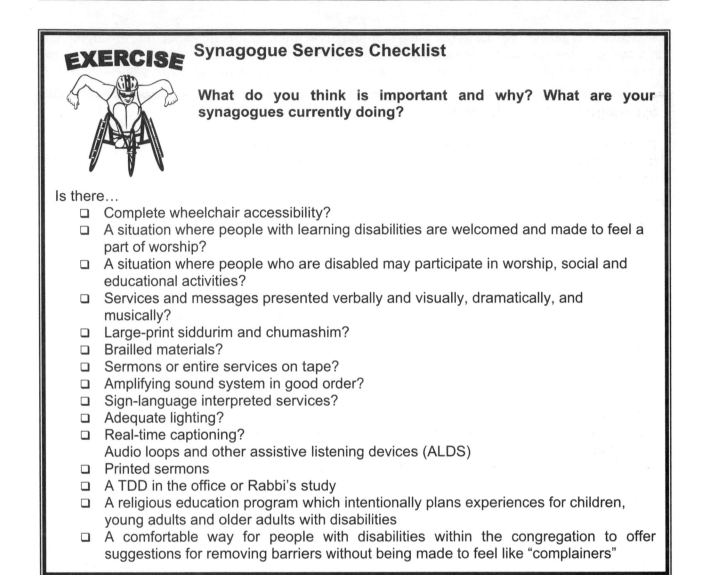

EXERCISE   Synagogue Services Checklist

What do you think is important and why? What are your synagogues currently doing?

Is there…
- ❏ Complete wheelchair accessibility?
- ❏ A situation where people with learning disabilities are welcomed and made to feel a part of worship?
- ❏ A situation where people who are disabled may participate in worship, social and educational activities?
- ❏ Services and messages presented verbally and visually, dramatically, and musically?
- ❏ Large-print siddurim and chumashim?
- ❏ Brailled materials?
- ❏ Sermons or entire services on tape?
- ❏ Amplifying sound system in good order?
- ❏ Sign-language interpreted services?
- ❏ Adequate lighting?
- ❏ Real-time captioning?
  Audio loops and other assistive listening devices (ALDS)
- ❏ Printed sermons
- ❏ A TDD in the office or Rabbi's study
- ❏ A religious education program which intentionally plans experiences for children, young adults and older adults with disabilities
- ❏ A comfortable way for people with disabilities within the congregation to offer suggestions for removing barriers without being made to feel like "complainers"

Architectural Barriers

When beginning to make the architectural and structural changes necessary to welcome people with disabilities, start with things that can be accomplished relatively easily. Get underway! What is needed are visible signs of change, not just lengthy committee meetings and hand-wringing.

It is true that aesthetic and historic preservation considerations must be taken into account as welcoming congregations make plans to adapt their buildings. And some of these adaptations will be expensive. It is not an acceptable argument, however, to delay because of "how few of them" we have. In God's realm, the number of users is not relevant.

Plan a fundraising strategy that involves everyone, young and old, rich and not so rich. Think about everything from bake sales and benefits to expensive physical changes made in loving memory of a deceased relative. In addition, remember that some religious groups grant low-interest loans for renovations.

Begin by consulting members of the congregation and their relatives who are architects, contractors, carpenters and plumbers. Their skills are needed and this is their day to shine! Don't forget to consult, in every phase of evaluation and planning, persons who are users of wheelchairs, walkers, crutches and canes. By not doing so, many churches and synagogues have made well-intended but inadequate, even wasteful, changes. It goes without saying that all new construction or remodeling should meet current local access codes.[xxxiv]

Synagogue Architectural Accessibility Checklist

Consider the architectural aspects of your congregation. Using the list below, see what has already been accomplished, and what they can still do.

APPROACH:
- ❑ Parking spaces are marked "Reserved for People with Disabilities."
- ❑ Spaces should be 12 feet wide to open door, and no loose gravel.
- ❑ Level approach to the synagogue; sidewalk to curb or curb ramps to the street.
- ❑ Ramps where there is a change in grade level and /or steps at some entrances.
- ❑ Ramps where steps are unavoidable. Multi-level buildings are barricades for some disabled unless modifications are made.
- ❑ Non-slip surface material, not heavy carpet should be used on ramps.
- ❑ Minimum ramp width of 36 inches.
- ❑ Rise of no more than one foot for 12 feet of ramp.
- ❑ Handrails should be 32-38 inches wide, and 30-32 inches high.
- ❑ Rails should be placed at inside/outside ramps.
- ❑ Rails should be placed at inside/outside steps, and steps to the bimah.
- ❑ Rails should be placed in traffic halls.
- ❑ Ramps should be placed in washrooms and toilets.

DOORS:
- ❑ Entry doors should be 36-38 inches wide.
- ❑ There should be at least one accessible entry door.
- ❑ Inside doors should be 30-32 inches clear opening.
- ❑ Doors swing without conflict with wheelchairs. It is easier to open a door inward.
- ❑ Vertical door handles or horizontal door bars should be used rather than slippery round knobs.
- ❑ Have blunt doorsills.
- ❑ Sliding doors should have recessed lower channel.

SANCTUARY:
- ❑ Accommodations for those on crutches or with walkers. One or two rows or seats or pews 36 inches apart.
- ❑ Scattered spaces or "pew cuts" for the users of wheelchairs who prefer to be seated in the main body of the congregration, not in the front or back of the sanctuary and not in the aisles.
- ❑ Non-Slip, non-glare floors.
- ❑ Bimah accessible to those with mobility impairments.
- ❑ Bookstands or lapboards available for those unable to hold siddurim or chumashim.
- ❑ Padded seats for some pews, or seat pads that can be handed out.

REST ROOMS:
- ❑ Entry 30-32 inches wide.
- ❑ At least one stall 5 feet deep, wide enough for a wheelchair 38 inches wide, and slide curtain or door that swings out.
- ❑ Grab bars in the toilet seat stall, 30 inches high, extending 24 inches from midway of the commode; in the urinal stall, the bar fixed vertically to stabilized one on crutches.
- ❑ One washbasin 30 inches high for wheelchairs.
- ❑ Faucets easily handled with one hand.
- ❑ Shelves should be installed to accommodate diabetic and ostomy supplies.

WATER FOUNTAINS:
- ❑ Spouts, controls up front.
- ❑ Placement not in alcove.
- ❑ Possibly install paper cup dispenser at the fountain.
- ❑ Hand or foot operated. Conventional water coolers can be improved by mounting a small fountain on the side, no more than 36 inches from the floor.

CORRIDORS:
- ❑ Corridors should be at least 36 inches wide. It takes at least 54 inches to turn a wheelchair.
- ❑ Floors should be non-slip.

TRANSPORTATION:
- ❑ Parking near entrance of building.
- ❑ Volunteer drivers and cars for synagogue activities.
- ❑ Volunteer drivers with vans with wheelchair ramps.
- ❑ Van with power lift for wheelchairs.

LIGHTING:
- ❑ Adequate light at book levels in all pews.
- ❑ Light from below the speaker's face to enliven and facilitate speech reading.
- ❑ Sight lines to speaker's face without glaring, bothersome lights.
- ❑ Sight lines to speaker's face without glaring window light.
- ❑ Braille siddurim and chumashim.
- ❑ Large print siddurim and chumashim for the partially sighted.

AMPLIFICATION:
- ❑ A good sound system, without dead spots.
- ❑ Earphones in some pews for hearing impaired.
- ❑ Possibility of an interpreter in sign language.

PREFACE

In regard to the issue of synagogue accessibility for persons with disabilities, the Committee on Jewish Law and Standards is working on a full detailed *teshuvah*. This will be released upon its approval by the Committee. Professor Joel Roth, the former chairman of the Committee, has written a letter, which deals with the question. Until the new responsum is approved, the letter of Professor Roth serves as a guide.

LETTER

December 27, 1988

Rabbi Stanley David
Central Synagogue
652 Lexington Avenue
New York, NY 10022

Dear Rabbi David:

The issue you raised with Rabbi David Lincoln has reached me in my capacity as chairman of the Committee on Jewish Law and Standards of the Rabbinical Assembly.

I find it hard to believe that designating the Central Synagogue as a landmark site would preclude installing an elevator intended to allow access to he synagogue by people with disabilities. Obviously, the talmudic courses could not refer to such a case because it is impossible to expect sages of 1500 years ago to deal with a reality they could not have dreamed of.

On the other hand, it seems clear to me that prohibiting the installation of an elevator in our time would be unethical and against Jewish law. People with disabilities are under no less legal obligation for communal prayer than are the able-bodied. When avenues exist for allowing them to avail themselves of the opportunity to pray with the community, or to participate in other synagogue activities, those avenues should be exploited to the fullest.

It seems to me that the increased sensitivity to he needs of people with disabilities which our generation is (thankfully) witnessing makes it virtually mandatory that a landmark site which is still in regular use be allowed to install an elevator. Surely, I suspect, this could be done in such a way as to leave the structure of the building only minimally modified. The designation as a landmark is intended to preserve the site even for the use and enjoyment of people with disabilities.

Sincerely yours,

Rabbi Joel Roth

OPENING THE GATES OF PRAYER . . . . SO THAT ALL MAY WORSHIP

by Shelley Kaplan[xxxv]

Today, some 54 million Americans -- one in five individuals -- have a disability. As a result, many of these people are prevented from worshiping within their religious community. For too many, the gates of prayer are closed due to structural, communicational, and attitudinal barriers. Obstacles to worship that alienate people with disabilities must be eliminated.

Accessible congregations promote acceptance and full participation of congregants with disabilities in all aspects of religious life. Installing ramps, increasing the number of accessible parking spaces, providing sign language interpreters and enlarging print materials are only some of the steps congregations must take to involve and include members with disabilities.

What's the Mitzvah?

When Moses stood before the burning bush, God said, "Take off your shoes from your feet, for the ground on which you are standing is holy unto me." What makes a space holy or spiritual? It was not just the space itself but the way Moses approached that space, or stood before it. Therefore, "approaches" to the synagogue attain a spiritual quality when they permit all to enter and to fully participate in worship and study.

It is a privilege to be called to the Torah for an *aliyah*. But what if one cannot navigate steps to access the *bimah*? What if a congregant cannot hear the Rabbi or Cantor? What if congregants with visual impairments cannot see the written prayers? According to Rabbi Arnold Goodman of Ahavath Achim Synagogue in Atlanta, Georgia, "No one should feel left out of our community and denied empowerment due to disability....Older Synagogues require more effort and ingenuity to effectively remove barriers. However, this challenge should be viewed as an investment." Judaism speaks of empowering the individual. Opening the gates of prayer so that all may worship is an important way to accomplish this goal.

What's the Problem?

According to a 1994 Louis Harris survey commissioned by the National Organization on Disability (N.O.D.) on the attitudes of people with disabilities, seven out of ten consider their religious faith to be very important. Most congregations work hard to be hospitable and welcoming, but the barriers which exclude children and adults with disabilities from full participation may not be easily understood or identified. Although many congregations have removed some of these barriers, few congregations have reached the "Promised Land" of access and welcome. Progress has been made in making facilities accessible -- enhanced lighting and sound systems, sign language interpreters, alternative text formats, access to the bimah, a reading table from which the Torah is read, microphones. Nevertheless, beliefs about physical and mental disabilities have been slower to change.

There is a pervasive belief that the best human beings are the strongest. We often do not realize that people with disabilities have gifts and talents to share with congregations. Identifying and discussing the unique abilities and needs of people with disabilities is an extremely important process for a congregation. Certainly, it is easier to add ramps, pew cuts, accessible parking places and restrooms than to remove the barriers of stereotypical thinking. These can be addressed through education (changing minds) and friendship (changing hearts).

What Have Other Synagogues Done?

Congregations throughout North America have taken steps to remove barriers to worship, whether architectural (ramps, handrails, wider doorways, grab bars in the restroom, accessible parking), communicative (assistive listening devices, sign language interpreters, large-print materials, braille *siddurim*) or attitudinal (education through disability awareness programs). The following congregations have been leaders in opening their gates of prayer.

Beth El Synagogue
Omaha, Nebraska

Rabbi Paul Drazen's vision was to build a synagogue that would express the spirit of the congregation and be viewed as a home by all of its members. He wanted a building that would be a distinguished addition to the Omaha landscape with a sanctuary in which communal worship could be fostered in a space that was warm, intimate and accessible.

"This vision", said architect Maurice Finegold, "begins with these intangibles and is mixed with an accumulated knowledge and philosophy, of building design in general and synagogue design in particular. We designed knowing that as members age, as new people come to the community, we had to be ready for them, because a synagogue that is not open, easily and without embarrassment, is not a synagogue for all."

The synagogue created a place for a sign language interpreter. A sound system to assist people with hearing impairments was installed. Pew cut-outs with book racks in front were created so that congregants in wheelchairs were afforded a variety of seating options. Not only were the steps leading to the *bimah* made wide for easy use, but a ramp was built as well. Throughout the building process, Rabbi Drazen kept in mind the teaching of the Torah that "we shall go forward with our young and our old," in order to ensure that everyone in Beth El would be included.

Adath Jeshurun
Elkins Park, Pennsylvania

Thanks to the dedication of Rabbi Seymour Rosenbloom and Congregational President Joseph Yohlin, Congregation Adath Jeshurun is fully accessible. In 1998, major additions, costing in excess of $80,000, were made in order to accommodate congregants with disabilities. To help disabled members reach a small auditorium located near the rear entrance from the parking lot, a wheelchair lift was installed next to the six steps. In 1997, during an extensive renovation to the main sanctuary, a ramp to the *bimah* was installed. Handrails to the *bimah* in both the sanctuary and the Chapel were also installed. An accessible shelf was inserted in the lectern so that the Torah could be lowered and the person receiving an *aliyah* would not have to stretch to make contact with the Scroll. Increased accessibility in the synagogue enabled a member who uses a wheelchair to participate in his nephew's Bar Mitzvah. "It made us feel good that he was able to have an *aliyah*; if we did not have the ramp, my brother-in-law's inability to participate would have left a void," said Gerald Klugman, father of the Bar Mitzvah.

Beth El Congregation
Phoenix, Arizona

In February 1994, Jay Dahsefsky was called to the Torah as a Bar Mitzvah. Seven very steep steps prevented him from reaching the Torah; unable to walk, Jay was carried to the *bimah* so that he could participate. When synagogue USYers conducted the Yom Kippur *Minha* service, this same seven-step barrier prevented Jay from equal participation. Rabbi Rick Sherwin dreamed of having a fully accessible sanctuary. In 1993, as a condition of employment, he insisted that the sanctuary be transformed within two years. As a result, during the summer of

1995, the sanctuary underwent major renovation with the express purpose of raising the floor, lowering the *bimah*, and placing a ramp so that all members could stand before the Torah. Architect Mo Stein designed a ramp which would not call attention to those using it and which afforded everyone dignity in approaching the Torah. On the Shabbat prior to Rosh Hashanah, the sanctuary re-opened and congregants who had never been able to come to the Torah were given that privilege. Jay Dashefsky, along with many others, were called up for an *aliyah* on this special Shabbat. "In every *simha*, we find someone who uses the ramp, and our congregation is no longer embarrassed by the exclusion of family members due to disability," said Rabbi Sherwin. "Everyone may now come to the *bimah* comfortably and with dignity."

Ahavath Achim Synagogue
Atlanta, Georgia

A prime example of an older synagogue committed to removing barriers, this historic congregation recently installed a wheelchair lift to its steep *bimah*. Located behind the *bimah*, individuals unable to navigate the steep steps can easily ascend in a dignified manner without drawing attention to themselves. "Having an *aliyah* on Yom Kippur made me feel like I still had value an a human being," said Sidney Kaplan, Past President, who uses a wheelchair for mobility following a stroke two years ago. A state-of-the-art assistive listening system enables numerous congregants to better participate in Shabbat services and family *simhas*. "For the first time, I was able to hear my niece chant Torah on her Bat Mitzvah", said a member with a severe hearing impairment.

Other accessibility features include a lectern for wheelchair users to read Torah, large-print *siddurim*, unisex accessible restroom, and increased accessible parking to accommodate people with disabilities and the elderly. Said Rabbi Arnold Goodman. "Cost cannot be used as an excuse for alienating any individual from prayer."

Congregation Ohev Shalom, Orlando, Florida

"Six months ago, two significant events occurred in my family's life. One was a family *simha* (the Bar Mitzvah of my oldest son) and the other was major back surgery for my father-in-law prior to the *simha*. These events intersected when it became apparent that my son's grandfather might not be able to climb the steps of our synagogue's *bimah* for his *aliyah*. Thus, building a ramp to the *bimah* became my son's Bar Mitzvah project." Utilizing a fund designed for increasing accessibility, augmented with money from the Bar Mitzvah fund, the project took off and the ramp was built, thanks to the assistance of a particular Hebrew teacher and his middle school students. "Our whole family was delighted with [such a] positive response from the congregation. We are pleased to know that a physical disability no longer precludes anyone in our synagogue from having an *aliyah* on our *bimah*", said Judy Levin, mother of the Bar Mitzvah.

What Is the United Synagogue Doing?

Many congregations throughout North America have opened their gates of prayer, however, many more do not know where to go for assistance. The United Synagogue seeks to identify and recognize the full range of congregations -- from those newly alerted to disability issues to those which are fully accessible. These congregations are being singled out for their commitment to action. The USCJ, through its Accessibility Committee, seeks to increase the level of religious participation of children and adults with disabilities by sharing information about what others have done in this area.

Two significant resolutions have been passed:

Mezuzah Accessibility -- drafted by USYers and adopted at 1997 United Synagogue Biennial Convention, the resolution calls upon all affiliated congregations to place the mezuzot low enough within the top third of the doorpost of the entrances to the synagogue to make them readily accessible to all and encouraging individuals to do the same in their homes.

Accessibility -- Enacted at its 1991 USCJ Biennial Convention, this resolution calls upon the USCJ to provide guidance to its constituent congregations for the implementation of measures to make synagogues accessible to persons with disabilities, urges all congregations to take immediate steps to make all synagogues physically and programmatically open and accessible to persons with disabilities, urges all segments of the congregation to become involved in the process of welcoming persons with disabilities into its synagogues, and commits to ensuring that all future conventions and public programs of the USCJ be held within facilities that provide adequate accessibility.

Mezuzah Accessibility (USYer's Resolution, adopted by USCJ in 1997)

Whereas, Jews are commanded (*Yoreh Deah* 289:6) to place a mezuzah on the top third of the door posts of their homes; and

Whereas, frequently *mezuzot* are placed so high within the top third of the door post that they are not accessible to young people and people with disabilities confined to wheelchairs; and

Whereas, placing the *mezuzah* lower within the top third of the doorpost is *halachically* permissible, and would enable all Jews to fulfill this mitzvah and would increase awareness in the community of the needs of those unable to reach the mezuzah;

Therefore be it resolved that the International USY Board calls upon the USY chapters to urge their congregations to place the *mezuzot* low enough within the top third of the door posts of the entrances to the synagogue to make them readily accessible to all and to encourage individuals to do the same in their homes.

WHAT YOU CAN DO?

Make a commitment to ensure your congregation is open to everyone who wants to worship. Start by:

- Acknowledging that barriers to full participation of people with disabilities may exist and make a commitment to begin the process of removing them.
- Educating rabbinical and lay leadership that people with disabilities are valued as individuals, having been created in the image of God.
- Removing barriers of architecture, communications and attitudes that exclude people with disabilities from full and active participation.
- Committing publicly to expanding efforts to welcome members and visitors with all types of disabilities. People, with and without disabilities, should be encouraged in your congregation to practice their faith and use their gifts in worship, service, study and leadership.
- Involving congregants with disabilities to serve on an Accessibility Committee. Members with disabilities are already accommodation experts. Once invited to participate, they will suggest low cost and practical solutions which others may have overlooked. People with disabilities and their family members, as well as congregants (who may be special education teachers, rehabilitation counselors, architects, builders, fundraisers, etc.) are the types of people who will be interested in working on this effort.
- Sharing your accessibility projects with USCJ. Your efforts will be recognized on USCJ's future web site. In this manner, others can learn by example and remove barriers in a meaningful and cost-effective manner.

For those in an older facility, the job of becoming truly accessible may seem overwhelming, but our tradition teaches us, "*Lo alecha hamlicha ligmor,*" that we must not allow the enormity of the task to prevent us from undertaking it. If we approach this task with a well-organized plan, we find that even our older buildings can be made highly accessible without outrageous expense or laborious effort. Here are some examples of "common sense" modifications:

> Instead of retrofitting both men's and women's restrooms to make them wheelchair accessible, select one restroom nearest the sanctuary to be adapted to become a unisex (or family) restroom which includes a wide stall, wheel-under sink and lowered towel dispenser. Besides the person who uses a wheelchair, this restroom benefits families with infants and small children in strollers.

> If you have a pay phone which is placed too high for a wheelchair user, the phone company will lower it to the appropriate height for you. Adding a chair nearby for unimpaired persons will make it more comfortable for them as well.

> Purchasing a TDD (telephone device for the deaf and disabled), a small modem which is plugged into any phone line, allows for ease of communication between those who are hard of hearing or deaf and your synagogue staff. It is inexpensive and easy to use.

> Building a ramp to the entrance of the building or to the bima is vital. In older buildings, you have several choices including building a permanent or portable ramp or purchasing a wheel- chair lift to place next to the bima. By providing an alternative to stairs, you provide assistance not just to those in wheelchairs but also to the elderly, those who use walkers, crutches or canes, and those who are

herding a family of children (including one in a stroller) into the building or up to the *bima* for a blessing.

LOW COST CHANGES FOR SYNAGOGUES

- PLASTIC MAGNIFYING SHEETS can be made available for use with your *siddurim* and *humashim*. Magnifying sheets can be sewn into covers in such a way that they can be placed over the pages in the book. This is an easy and cost-effective way to provide for those who need large-print books.

- LOWER THE Mezuzah on the entrance to your Synagogue so it is reachable by everyone including people in wheelchairs. *Mezuzah* Accessibility—drafted by USYers and adopted at the 1997 United Synagogue Biennial Convention, the resolution calls upon all affiliated congregations to place the *mezuzot* low enough within the top third of the doorpost of the entrances to the synagogue to make them readily accessible to all and encouraging individuals to do the same in their homes.

- LOWER YOUR BOX OF KIPPOT so that they are reachable by everyone including people in wheelchairs.

- PROVIDE ACCESSIBLE PARKING SPACES that are reserved for people who use wheelchairs or cannot walk long distances to the Synagogue's entrance.

- EDUCATE USHERS about the various accessibility features offered by you Synagogue. This knowledge goes a long way to creating a welcoming environment for people who benefit from your barrier removal efforts.

- MOUNT A CUP DISPENSER next to your water fountain as a low cost alternative to purchasing a new one that is accessible. Make sure it is mounted at a height convenient for use by persons in wheelchairs. It is also important that cups be maintained in the dispenser.

- IMPROVE YOUR SYNAGOGUE'S AIR QUALITY by dusting woodwork/brass in the sanctuary, vacuuming with a HEPA filter and cleaning air conditioning filters on a routine basis.

- POST APPROPRIATE SIGNAGE indicating the location of your accessible entrance, path of travel and restrooms.

SABBATH IN A BOX

A great idea comes from the American Association on Mental Retardation called "Sabbath in a box". The idea is to enable someone who is disabled to join his/her religious community in the celebration of the Sabbath or a festival. Boxes are prepared with a pair of candlesticks and 6 candles, a wine cup and small bottle of grape juice, head-coverings appropriate to a man or woman, a *challah* and a *challah* cover, a *tzedakah* box, and other items. There is an instruction manual including an explanation of Shabbat and some of the major readings and prayers. An audio cassette tape includes prayers and songs in Hebrew and English.

These boxes are personally delivered to the people who need them by a volunteer. Together they decorate the unadorned *challah* cover. Thus, the Shabbat items are provided as well as personal companionship.

WHY BOTHER?

Ultimately we must come to see that making room in our society and in our synagogues for those with disabilities is in our own best interest. Think back to the *Midrashim* which spoke of the "insight" of those who are blind and the teaching of people who are deaf. We are more enriched to the degree that we open our doors to people with disabilities, for at least two reasons. First, out of a sense of fairness and justice, we should not exclude members of our community from participating with us. Secondly, there are many instances in which a disability can be an advantage.

SOME CURRENT PROGRAMS
THE HEVRAH PROGRAM OF FAR WEST USY

In 1996, the Far West region of USY, working in concert with Camp Ramah in California, founded the Hevrah Program for Jewish teens with special needs. The Hevrah Program, which has been built upon the foundation of the Tikvah "Buddy Program" at Camp Ramah, brings together participants and active USYers for socialization, religious educational programming and their own social action programming. While the Tikvah Buddy Program takes place only during the summer at camp, the Hevrah Program is available year-round and draws participants from Los Angeles, Orange, San Bernardino and Ventura Counties.

Each year, the Hevrah Program begins with a USYer orientation consisting of sensitivity-building workshops, led by special educational professionals, containing simulation exercises about living with special needs. The current program includes over 75 teenagers with special needs including over participants not necessarily involved in the Tikvah program. In order to encourage the development of long-lasting friendships, each USYer is assigned a Hevrah buddy. At each event, the buddies have time to interact, participate in group activities and work on the development of team building and trust skills. Jewish holiday celebrations, social action projects and arts and crafts are also part of the programming mix. A Hevrah Shabbaton is the culmination program where all of the participants join together for a wonderful weekend together.

L'Taken Olam-- Bridging the Gap:

Emtza USY

In 1999, Emtza Region USY began a unique partnership with the Camp Ramah in Wisconsin Tikvah program for campers with special needs. Emtza Region reached out to those USYers with special needs who were formerly not involved with their chapters or the region. USYers with special needs began to attend regional events, and in turn, began to attend chapter events and get involved in their local youth programs. The Tikvah program has provide Emtza with a source of trained, qualified staff to deal with these teenagers' special needs. In turn, these teenagers, who have had positive experiences at regional events, oftentimes become involved in their local chapters.

> I'm proud to be Jewish and I'm proud of the way that Jewish people treat other people. My Camp Ramah experience and the USY weekends have shown me that I'm a good person, despite being a little different than anyone else. We all have or unique abilities. I am so thankful to Camp Ramah and USY for giving me the opportunity to be around other Jewish people."
> —Mitch Paschen, Baraboo, WI

Emtza currently has approximately eight-ten USYers with special needs at each regional event. These USYers were made to feel welcome in the region and a part of the program. They had staff that were brought in especially to serve as their advocates. The USYers with special needs participated fully in the Emtza program, and many of them went back to their hometowns enthused about being a part of USY and being Jewish.

Emtza has also begun a program geared towards former USYers with special needs who have already completed high school. In this new vocational program, these former USYers receive further opportunities to attend conventions as staff members. They, too, have benefited from their ongoing involvement with USY.

Tikvah Program of Camp Ramah

In 1969 the United Synagogue Commission on Jewish Education for the Special Child suggested to the National Ramah Commission that a Ramah camp sponsor a special education program. The program began with Herb Greenberg as the first Tikvah Director:[xxxvi]

> Three months were available to organize a group and hire a staff for the 1970 inaugural program. More than one hundred congregations were contacted in the northeast, and rabbis and congregational leaders were asked to submit the names of families with handicapped adolescents. Rabbinical and Jewish educational leaders had limited information to offer at the time. In most situations the Tikvah Director and camp representatives were put in touch with members of a congregation who were mental health professionals, or agencies which were providing services for the handicapped and their families.

Finally, the first group of eight youngsters, ranging in age from 13 to 17, was identified. It came as no surprise that most of those youngsters were denied Jewish education and that their families were discouraged from pursuing Bar or Bat-Mitvah preparations. That first summer, the Tikvah Program began to provide training for Bar and Bat-Mitzvah completion.

Since its inception, much has been accomplished. The Jewish community is fully aware of the religious educational needs of these youngsters and almost every Jewish community has a congregation which provides programs of special education. For many summers, it was quite common to confirm five or six Tikvah youngsters at the camp. Today, the Jewish community has assumed this obligation, and there are few Tikvah *B'nai* or *B'not Mitzvah* during the summer months.

Now special needs programs have spread to other Ramah camps. Five camps, located in Massachusetts, New York, Wisconsin, California, and Canada, have programs that serve populations of Jewish adolescents who have developmental delays, mental retardation, autism/ Asperger's Syndrome, Down Syndrome and other handicapping conditions that prevent them from functioning in camp without significant additional supports.

"I can't tell you the pride, joy and gratitude we all felt. Brian was so thrilled that he almost burst. In between some serious *davening*, he blew kisses to his fans, raised his *t'fillin*-wrapped arm in a two-fingered salute, shook hands, and accepted congratulations somewhere between an accomplished bar mitzvah boy and a Hollywood celebrity! The whole camp cheered in one voice when he succeeded in articulating his solos.

I never thought I would say this, but my son is happier in some place other than home. It is quite miraculous when 'potential' becomes a word in the present tense. For a few hours, we really felt the meaning of true inclusiveness. When we left Ramah, we knew it was possible for Brian to be not just a man, but a mensch, in his own community."

Mother of Tikvah camper, upon celebration of his Bar Mitzvah.

At Camp Ramah in California, Camp Ramah in New England,and Camp Ramah in Wisconsin, Tikvah campers are placed in special programs that allow them to integrate into camp activities whenever possible, with appropriate supports, and special educational and social skill development. Camp Ramah in the Berkshires provides Briera B'Ramah for campers with special needs, mainstreaming these campers into camper bunks. Ramah's newest program for children with special needs is Camp Yofi, a week-long family camp based at Ramah Darom in Georgia. Ramah Day in Chicago also offers programming for children with special needs.

Camp Netaim of the Ramah-NOAM Summer Camp in Israel[xxxvii]

As a natural continuation of the Bar/Bat Mitzvah for the Special Child program, in which children with special needs study Jewish values and observance, the Masorti Movement offers a rich informal educational opportunity at the Ramah-NOAM Summer Camp. As with all other groups, the camp experience for these children reinforces their understanding of Jewish tradition and their sense of connection with Jewish peers and with the Jewish community. The combining of the two camps creates a wonderful opportunity for Tikun Olam (social action), for all involved.

First held during the summer of 1999, Camp Netaim has been extraordinarily successful, and has become a permanent feature of the Ramah-NOAM Summer Camp, which attracts almost 500 children. Growing from a one-week program, Netaim campers now experience two full weeks of fun and educational activities, often participating in programs of Ramah-NOAM.

Bar/ Bat Mitzvah Program in Israel for Special Needs Child[xxxviii]

The Bar/Bat Mitzvah for the Special Child program annually prepares over 300 children with special needs for their Bar or Bat Mitzvah ceremony. Since 1995, the Masorti Movement has been running Israel's only national Bar/Bat Mitzvah program, which reaches out systematically to children with special needs in Israeli schools. Originally starting in one school, today the program operates in forty schools, hospitals and institutions throughout Israel and educates some 300 children a year.

The program works with youth with special needs who would not otherwise benefit from Jewish enrichment classes, and provides an opportunity for them to be called up to the Torah. Participants include children with a variety of special needs, including those with Cerebral Palsy, Down syndrome, mild and moderate mental retardation, hearing impairments, ADD, ADHD and other behavioral challenges, autism, and blindness. No one is turned away on the basis of the severity of his or her disability. About one third of the participants are new immigrants.

The Bar/Bat Mitzvah for the Special Child reaches out to all sectors of the community (Orthodox, Reform, Masorti, secular, new immigrants), offering every child the opportunity to experience this important life-cycle event. The program attempts to re-enter these children into society as "whole people with varying differences," providing both children and families with the pride and joy of accomplishing this Jewish crossroads in their lives.

No other organization offers such a systematic teaching program for this sector of Israeli society, the overwhelming majority of which would otherwise not have the opportunity for a Bar or Bat Mitzvah. This project continues to ensure that one more section of our society, children with special needs, is included within the Jewish fold.

SENSITIVITY

Perhaps the following guidelines will be useful in helping us better know how to be sensitive to the needs and feelings of those who are disabled and caring for them. The material is from the New York State Office of Advocate for people with disabilities, reprinted with permission.

Communication: A Two Way Street

If you are not used to communicating with a person who has a disability and have any hesitations or concerns, here are a few tips:

- **USE COMMON SENSE**. People with disabilities want to be treated the same way as everyone else.
- **BE POLITE**. Show the person the same respect that you would expect to the given you.
- **BE CONSIDERATE**. Be patient, take time and try to understand the problem or need of the individual.
- **OFFER ASSISTANCE**. Do not hesitate to offer assistance. However, do not automatically give help unless the person clearly needs help or asks for it. If the person declines your help, do not insist on helping. Ask the person if assistance is needed and how it should be given.

- **COMMUNICATE**. Talk directly to the person. It is not difficult to communicate with a disabled person. In some cases, it may take a little time, depending on the person's disability.
- **EMERGENCY ACTION**. Know the location of disabled individuals in your building to help with evacuation, if necessary, during an emergency.

CONCLUDING NOTE FROM THE EDITOR

In the times that the Rabbis were discussing whether to include—and *how* to include— people with disabilities, the words they used were acceptable. Twenty years ago when this book was first published, the terminology within it was current and up-to-date. The further we delve into the topic of disabilities, the more we uncover. Twenty years from now, the terminology within this book will be outdated and the words we used will be deemed insensitive. Unlike other topics, this one deals with people who are continuously trying to define themselves in ways that reflect their inner-souls, and not just what is confronted from the outside.

As you move through the final sections of this book, please think carefully about how you can incorporate aspects of this chapter into your lives. In *Pirke Avot* we learn that we do not have to complete the task, but nor are we free to avoid it. We need to continuously strive to make our congregations accessible and our homes welcoming to persons with disabilities. We need to make a promise to advocate and be thoughtful. We need to make a promise to be to each other, as we would want to be treated ourselves.

K.L.S.

APPENDIX A: OFFERING ASSISTANCE[xxxix]

Here are some helpful pointers to keep in mind when you are trying to decide whether or not to provide assistance.

1. It is okay to offer assistance

Like everyone, there are times when a person with a disability wants assistance and there are times when they don't. Everyone appreciates some assistance now and then. And most people, including people with disabilities, like to assist someone once in a while.

While it is appropriate to offer assistance, it is not appropriate to spontaneously provide assistance. Doing so assumes that the person with a disability needs or wants it. Never assume someone needs or wants your assistance.

Remember Rule 2: When in doubt ASK

2. Ask before providing assistance

When you don't want or need assistance, the last thing you want is someone "helping" you. Before assisting a person with a disability, ask them whether or not they would like assistance. They may say "yes" or "no." The important thing is to let the person with the disability make the decision.

3. Clarify what type of assistance is desired

Everyone has their own way of doing things.

Some ways work better than others. Before assisting a person with a disability, ask them how you can best assist. Let them tell you how they would like to be assisted.

These basic ideas apply to interacting with persons with all kinds of disabilities, whether they are people with mobility disabilities, people with hearing disabilities, people with vision disabilities, people with communication disabilities, people with mental disabilities, substance abuse, or other health conditions such as arthritis, multiple sclerosis, AIDS, cancer, etc.

PEOPLE WITH MOBILITY DISABILITIES

<u>Just the Facts</u>

1. Signs, signs, everywhere are signs

Almost everywhere you go now-a-days you can see the international symbol of accessibility (the white wheelchair figure on a blue background). You see it in parking areas, restrooms, and on the front of buildings. However, increased awareness doesn't necessarily result in increased accessibility. These signs can be very misleading.

While a few genuinely accessible facilities do exist, a majority of facilities and services identified with an "accessible" symbol are not. The white and blue symbol of accessibility doesn't assure that facilities actually are accessible.

For example:

"Handicapped Parking"

Many "handicapped" parking spaces are inaccessible. While they may be reserved for persons with disabilities, their size or location can actually impair a person's ability to get in and out of their car.

Accessible parking spaces are supposed to be 13 feet wide. The additional width is necessary to get a car door open wide enough to get in and out of the car or to use an electric lift for getting in and out of a van.

When was the last time you saw a "handicapped" parking space that was a minimum of 13 feet wide?

"Access Ramps"
Ramps are supposed to have a slope no greater than 1 inch of height for every 12 inches of length. Not all ramps meet this requirement and therefore are not accessible. When a ramp with a slope steeper than the 1- to 12-inch requirement is referred to as "accessible," it is very misleading and can be potentially dangerous.

2. My Chair, My Body
A wheelchair or a walker may look like just another piece of equipment. However, people who use a wheelchair, walker, or cane often consider this technology as an extension of their body. Wheelchairs are NOT footstools, stepladders, or fire hazards. They are part of a person's person and should be treated with the same dignity and respect.

Touching or handling someone's wheelchair or other mobility tool may be seen as the same as touching or handling the person's body and may be considered inappropriate without the permission of the individual.

Myth Blasting
- The international symbol of accessibility does not assure that a building or activity is accessible.
- Touching or handling a person's wheelchair, walker, or other mobility device can be the same as touching their body.
- People with paralysis can and do have children.
- Having a mobility disability does NOT mean that you have other disabilities.
- Using a wheelchair or other mobility device does NOT constitute an inability to achieve a fulfilling life and a satisfying lifestyle.

Etiquette
1. Talk face to face
Be sure to face a person with a disability when talking to them. Carrying on a conversation with someone from behind, especially if you're standing over them, isn't very respectful of their dignity.

2. Look me in the eye when you say that
Quite often people who use wheelchairs have to look up at the person who is talking to them. This puts a strain on the person who is forced to look up at the person talking. This may also communicate an unequal status. Try to establish level eye contact by getting a chair and sitting down.

3. Empathetic mumbo-jumbo
Don't feel compelled to communicate your empathic impressions of what it must be like to use a wheelchair.

Having had a temporary disability, or having known a relative who used a wheelchair, may give you an experience with using a wheelchair or knowing someone who did; however, it does not tell you about someone else's experience.

Each person's experience is different. There are people who would say being in a wheelchair is the best thing that ever happened to them. There are other people who wouldn't agree.
If you're trying to bridge any social distance you might feel, talk about something that you both have in common like work, recreation, sports, etc.

Words
Words are very powerful. Think about these typical phrases:

"Confined to a wheelchair" -- This author doesn't know of anyone who is absolutely, totally confined to a wheelchair by ropes, chains or a court order.
"Wheelchair bound" -- When the author hears this term, he is reminded of an image where a person is crawling towards their chair singing "Hi, ho, hi, ho it's off to chair I go...."
"Wheelchair Person" -- When the author hears this term, he thinks of a wheelchair which has eyes, ears, a nose and a mouth. This term will dehumanize the person.

Use words that promote the personhood and abilities of the individual rather than a device they use or a physical limitation they have. For example:
"A person with a mobility disability" or "A person with a disability"

PEOPLE WITH HEARING DISABILITIES
Just the Facts
1."Hearing disability," "hard of hearing," and "deaf" mean different things
Most people think that "hearing disability," "hard of hearing," and "deaf" refer to the same thing. They don't. The term "hearing disability" refers to persons who are hard of hearing AND persons who are deaf.

Persons who are deaf and persons who are hard of hearing feel it is important to be recognized for their distinctive differences. An agreement between the World Federation of the Deaf and the International Federation of the Hard of Hearing has defined the difference between "deaf" and "hard of hearing."

The distinction is that "deaf people seek to utilize their vision skills for communicating while hard of hearing persons seek ways to retain their listening and speaking skills. Therefore, their concerns, needs, and emphases are different."

The range of hearing disabilities, like other disabilities, is composed of a variety of types and degrees. A person who is hard of hearing may hear only specific pitches, high or low, or a specific range of tones in between. (Think of the octaves on a piano.) Hard of hearing may also refer to volume. Persons who are hard of hearing may only hear loud sounds.

People who have some hearing may choose to rely more on speech for communicating. People who are deaf may choose to rely on Sign Language for communication. It is important to understand that a hearing loss may affect people differently.

2. All hard of hearing and deaf people do not read lips

One of the greatest fallacies regarding persons who are hard of hearing or deaf is that they speech read lips very well. Research indicates that less than thirty percent of spoken English sounds are visible, and that fifty percent of English sounds look like another sound on the lips.

3. Most deaf people have some vocal capacity

Another myth about deaf people is they can't vocalize. Most deaf people have normal vocal organs and can vocalize. However, because of cultural issues, a lack of auditory cues, role models, or training, deaf people may choose not to vocalize.

4.Communication used by deaf people

Deaf people use a variety of ways to communicate. They may choose to speak, speech read, write, or use a variety of "signed communication." Signed communication is a term referring to the use of fingerspelling (manually spelling letters with your fingers), American Sign Language, or a variety of signed English systems. These have different grammatical structures and may be mixed together.

American Sign Language (ASL) is the definitive language of the deaf culture and is used by many deaf people throughout the United States and parts of Canada. Like all natural languages, ASL has its own rules for grammar and conversational structures to convey information and ideas.

Myth Blasting

- Hard of hearing does not mean deaf.
- All people who are deaf or hard of hearing can NOT read lips.
- Most deaf people have normal vocal organs and can vocalize.
- Some deaf people DO have excellent speech.
- Finger spelling is NOT the same as Sign Language.
- Many deaf or hard of hearing enjoy music, theater, and movies.
- Being deaf or hard of hearing does NOT mean that you have other disabilities.
- Being deaf or hard of hearing does NOT constitute an inability to achieve a fulfilling life and a satisfying lifestyle.

Etiquette
1. Communicating with a TDD or TT

"TDD" stands for "Telecommunication Device for the Deaf" and may also be referred to as a "TT" for "Text Telephone." Either term is acceptable and refers to a small compact device that looks like a small typewriter keyboard with an LED screen. You type messages using the keyboard and read messages from the screen.

When typing your message on the TDD, make your communication clear, simple, and concise. When reading messages, be aware that abbreviations and ASL grammar may make the translation take a little longer. Try to focus on the whole message being conveyed, rather than trying to figure out individual words or phrases.

You need to know the abbreviations GA, Q and SK when communicating via a TDD. Type "GA" (go ahead) when you want the other person to start typing. When you read "GA," it is your turn to type. When you ask a question, type "Q" instead of a question mark. Type "SK" when you want to conclude your conversation. When you read "SK," type "SKSK" if you are completely finished talking. When both you and the person you are talking to have typed "SK," your conversation has ended and you can hang-up your phone and turn off your TDD.

If you work or live in a place that has telephones and TDDs and you answer a ringing phone and hear a beeping sound or silence, DON'T hang-up, it may be a TDD call. If you know how to use a TDD, answer the call. If you don't know how to use a TDD, find someone who can answer the call, or use a telephone relay system. Just DON'T hang-up. Don't type your message while the other person is typing their message. Only one person at a time can type and send their message via a TDD over the phone.

2. Using an interpreter

Always, always address your comments, questions, and concerns directly to the deaf person to whom you are talking. Even if you are using an interpreter, speak directly to the person with the hearing disability. Treat the interpreter as a foreign language translator; that's their role, nothing more.

Never talk to the interpreter or solicit information about the deaf person from the interpreter. Look at and communicate directly to the deaf person. The interpreter's job is to translate language, not interpret, mediate, or negotiate.

For example, do NOT speak to the interpreter and say, "Ask him where he would like to sit." Instead, speak directly to the person you are talking to and say, "Mr. Johnson, where would you like to sit?"

Always use a qualified interpreter. Never use someone who knows "a little" sign language. Using someone who knows a little sign language is like using a foreign language interpreter who knows just a little English.

Words

Never use the word "dumb" to denote a person who is hard of hearing or deaf. Use words which appropriately describe the person's abilities, such as, "a person who is hard of hearing." Remember that "the deaf" or "deaf person" is an exception to this rule. The terms "the deaf" or "deaf person" are preferred by national organizations of persons who are deaf.

PEOPLE WITH VISION DISABILITIES

Just the Facts
1. Blind doesn't mean blind

One of the most common myths about persons with vision disabilities is that they live in a world of total darkness. The range of vision disabilities, like other disabilities, is varied. For example, some people have peripheral vision while others have central vision. Some people have clouded vision while others may have multiple vision. Some people have a combination of many types of vision.

The concept of darkness is not relevant to most persons with vision disabilities. Someone who has no vision at all may not "see" any darkness.

2. SUPERSENSES is super-senseless

Having a vision disability does not give someone super-hearing, super-smell, super-taste, or super-touch. Persons with vision disabilities may learn to pay more attention to their other senses. However, paying closer attention to other senses is learned. The other senses do not "become" super senses.

The senses of a person with a vision disability are not naturally heightened as a result of their vision disability.

3. Persons with vision disabilities have strengths and weaknesses like everyone else
People who are blind or have a vision disability may have a very good sense of their location and direction as they are traveling. Having a vision disability doesn't automatically mean that someone needs assistance. Some people who are blind are very good navigators in familiar surroundings where they live, work, and play. Other people who are blind may not have developed these skills. Like everyone else, persons with disabilities will vary in their interests, skills, and abilities.

Myth Blasting
- Having a vision disability does NOT mean a person lives in total darkness.
- Having a vision disability does not GIVE someone super-hearing, super-smell, super-taste, or super-touch.
- Having a vision disability does NOT mean you do not know where you are or where you want to go. Having a vision disability, or being blind, does NOT mean that you have other disabilities.
- Having a vision disability does NOT constitute an inability to achieve a fulfilling life and a satisfying lifestyle.

Etiquette
1. Memory games are rude
Always identify yourself verbally when addressing a person with a vision disability. Most people with vision disabilities find it very rude and impolite to have someone come up to them and say, "Do you remember my voice?"

2. Communication
For some reason persons with vision disabilities are often shouted at. (Interestingly, this behavior contradicts the myth of super-hearing.) Use your normal tone of voice; don't shout.
It is okay to use vision references such as "see" or "look."

3. Orientation
It is considered polite to indicate your position with a light tap on the shoulder or hand (as in the case of a handshake or when offering mobility assistance). However, keep your physical contact reserved.

It is very important to identify yourself when you approach a person with a vision disability and to tell them when you are leaving the conversation or area.

4. Assistance
For mobility assistance, the best practice is to offer your elbow and allow the person with the vision disability to direct you when assisting him/her with their mobility. Don't push, don't propel, or grab the person or any part of their body and attempt to lead them; groping is quite impolite.

5. Service animals
A guide dog, like all service animals, should never be petted or talked to without the permission of its owner. Guide dogs, when in harness, are working and should not be distracted.

Words

Avoid cliches' where "blind" is used to mean "stupid," such as:

- The blind leading the blind.
- What are you ... blind?
- I'm not "blind" you know.

Use words which convey the abilities and wholeness of the person.

- Person with a vision disability.
- Person who is blind.

PEOPLE WITH COMMUNICATION DISABILITIES

Just the Facts

Speech disabilities range from problems with articulation, or voice strength, to complete voicelessness. They include difficulties in projection, as in chronic hoarseness and esophageal speech; fluency problems, as in stuttering and stammering; and the nominal aphasia that alters the articulation of particular words or terms.

1. I can speak for myself

Having a communication disability does not mean that a person does not desire to speak for himself. Most persons with communication disabilities do wish to speak for themselves. However, more often than not, other people feel compelled to try to speak for them. In most cases, "normal" people do not give the person with the communication disability the time they need to speak for themselves.

2. Not having clear speech does not mean I'm stupid

If a person has difficulty communicating verbally it does not mean that he is not capable of thinking for himself. Having difficulty speaking does not mean a person is unintelligent.

3. Avoidance is the number one response

The number one issue that people with communication disabilities have regarding communicating with other people is patience. Generally speaking, most people aren't willing to give people with communication disabilities the time they need to send their message. It seems that most people exercise avoidance or impatience when interacting with a person with a communication disability.

4. Telephone Avoidance

Communicating to another person on the telephone can be a nightmare for a person with a communication disability. Persons with communication disabilities reported that when they make a phone call the people who answer the phone usually take action which immediately ends the conversation.

For example, most people would:

    a. Immediately say, "I can't understand you." and/or
    b. Put them on hold, and/or
    c. Promptly refer the call to their supervisor

5. Listening pays off

In most cases, persons with communication disabilities can be understood if the listener takes the time to listen to what they have to say.

In conducting interviews with persons with severe communication disabilities for this handbook, the author was surprised by the ease with which he was able to understand what people were saying after two to four minutes of attentive listening.

Myth Blasting

- Having slow speech, or any speech difference, does not mean you can't or don't want to talk for yourself.
- Slow speech does not equal a slow mind.
- Having a communication disability does not mean a person is drunk.
- Having a communication disability does NOT mean that you have other disabilities.
- Having slow or difficult speech does NOT constitute an inability to achieve a fulfilling life and a satisfying lifestyle.

Etiquette

1. Take time, relax, and listen

Be patient, give the person the time they desire to be able to speak for themselves. Focus your attention on what is being communicated. Don't be afraid that you can't deal with the person who has a communication disability. With a little time and patience, you can comfortably converse with a person with a communication disability.

Trying to rush the conversation or second guess what a person has to say may only increase their stress and reduce effective communication. Speed is not the goal. If you push for quick answers, it can make it more difficult for the person with the communication disability to answer.

2. It's okay to say, "I don't understand"

It is okay to say, "I don't understand," if you have given someone the time and patience they require to send their message.

3. Solicit and provide feedback

If necessary, repeat your understanding of the message in order to clarify and/or confirm what was said. Or, ask to have information repeated. Sometimes spelling words can be helpful.

If you are experiencing some difficulty communicating, explain what you would like to do to facilitate the communication. Be sure to solicit feedback on your proposed solution before taking action.

4. Reduce or eliminate background noise

By reducing or eliminating background noise, it may be easier to focus on the conversation.

5. Treat persons with communication disabilities with dignity and respect; listen to their words

Don't engage in avoidance responses like:

a. Immediately putting them on hold.

b. Immediately getting someone else to talk with them.

c. Immediately saying "I don't understand."

d. Asking to talk to someone else about what the person with the communication disability may need or want.

6. Encourage the use of a telephone relay system if they do not use a TDD or TT

Words

Don't use language which focuses attention on the disability, such as:

- Slurred speech
- Unintelligible speech

Use words which more appropriately put the disability into perspective:
- Person with a communication disability
- Person with slow speech
- Person who uses artificial speech

PEOPLE WITH LEARNING DISABILITIES

Just the Facts
1. May be a "hidden" disability.
2. People with learning disabilities often have average to superior intelligence. They are NOT slow, lazy, or unmotivated.
3. Learning disabilities are a group of conditions (probably neurological in origin) that cause significant difficulties in perception. The particular disability might be in the area of auditory, visual, or spatial perception.
4. Learning disabilities may affect writing (dysgraphia), reading (dyslexia), mathematics (dyscalculia), listening comprehension, and/or oral expression.
5. Learning disabilities cause significant discrepancy between intellectual capacity and individual achievement.
6. The type of accommodation and learning strategies vary with the exact nature of the individual's disability. Additionally, when the person with a learning disability has an oral language deficit, it is difficult for them to express their needs.

Myth Blasting
- People with learning disabilities are NOT unintelligent.

Etiquette
1. Do NOT assume a person with a learning disability is a slow learner or performer.
2. Learn about the individual's strengths and weaknesses.
3. Ask for the individual's assistance in planning accommodations.

PEOPLE WITH PSYCHIATRIC DISABILITIES

Just the Facts
1. There are many different types of psychiatric illnesses, and each individual diagnosis is determined by a variety of factors.

2. The wide range of behaviors associated with mental illness may vary from indifference to disruptiveness. When the illness is active, the individual may or may not be at risk of harming himself or others.

3. The wide range of behaviors include, but are not limited to: depression, feelings of hopelessness, sadness, apathy, inattention, poor concentration, fatigue, sleep or eating disturbances, anxiety, withdrawal, constant talking, joking, fantasizing, or extreme fear or panic.

4. Many psychiatric disabilities are controlled by medication and have little effect on learning. However, many medications have side effects which may cause drowsiness or disorientation, and may also affect learning.

Myth Blasting

- People who have a psychiatric illness DO NOT have a cognitive disability.
- People with a psychiatric disability are NOT "crazy."

PEOPLE WITH EPILEPSY

Just the Facts

1. Also known as a "seizure disorder," characterized by a sudden overload of electrical energy in the brain.

2. Seizures may range from "absence" (formerly called petit mal) to "generalized" (formerly called grand mal).

3. Most (approximately 65%) seizure disorders are controlled with medication, and most have infrequent seizures while on medication.

Myth Blasting

- A person cannot swallow his/her tongue during a seizure.
- People who have epilepsy are not violent against themselves or others during a seizure. But, certain safety precautions should be taken so that no one is hurt accidentally.
- When a person is having a seizure you should NOT place anything in his/her mouth.
- Epilepsy does NOT prevent people from participating in sports, work, or social activities.

Etiquette

1. Education about seizures will reduce fear and myths.
2. Discuss with the person with a seizure disorder their particular needs.
3. Assist during a seizure by protecting the individual from environmental safety hazards (move sharp objects, place pillow under head).

APPENDIX B -- RESOURCE LIST

This list, while far from complete, references some of the organizations that are specifically advocating and providing services for Jewish people with disabilities.

MATAN: The Gift of Jewish Learning for Every Child (www.matankids.org)
MATAN is committed to giving the gift of Jewish learning to every child regardless of ability. Our fundamental educational philosophy is that all children learn differently and some learners need additional resources to succeed in their academic environments. Jewish education often presents challenges to children with special learning needs. By providing support to children, teachers and families, MATAN aims to address these challenges one child at a time.

The Jewish Guild for the Blind (The Guild), (www.jgb.org), is a not-for-profit, non-sectarian agency that serves persons of all ages who are visually impaired, blind and multidisabled. The Guild offers a broad range of programs that include: medical, vision, low vision, psychiatric and rehabilitative services, managed long-term care, residential services, day health programs, schools and educational training programs for independent living. Their mission is to assist people who are blind or visually impaired, and who may have additional disabilities, achieve lives of dignity and independence.

The Jewish Braille Institute (www.jewishbraille.org) counsels the families of blind, visually impaired children and reading disabled children. The JBI prepares the Braille, Audio and Large Print books necessary for a complete education as well as liturgical and life cycle materials in Braille, Audio and Large Print.

The Jewish Deaf Resource Center (www.jdrc.org) Founded by two young women in 1996-- one Deaf and one hearing—who dreamed the Jewish Deaf can participate in and shape the rich worlds of Jewish liturgy, education, culture, and communal life on an equal basis with hearing Jews.

Jewish Deaf Congress (www.jdcc.org) (Formerly National Congress of Jewish Deaf) Advocates for religious, educational, and cultural ideals and fellowship for Jewish deaf people. Conducts workshops for rabbi, parents of deaf children, and interpreters. Works with 20 affiliates and maintains a Hall of Fame.

Camp Ramah – Tikvah Program: (www.campramah.org/tikvah.html) Five camps, located in Massachusetts, New York, Wisconsin, California, and Canada, have programs that serve populations of Jewish adolescents who have developmental delays, mental retardation, autism/Asperger's Syndrome, Down Syndrome and other handicapping conditions that prevent them from functioning in camp without significant additional supports.

United Synagogue of Conservative Judaism, Committee on Accessibility
(www.uscj.org/accessibility/) maintains an advocacy website including resources and articles on disabilities.

United Synagogue of Conservative Judaism, Department of Education, (www.uscj.org) has materials and information available for teaching children with disabilities. For consultations and referral contact Department of Education, 155 Fifth Avenue, New York, NY 10010, 212-533-7800 x 2509, e-mail: Education@uscj.org and/or your United Synagogue Regional office.

Shalva (www.shalva.org) Providing SHALVA-PEACE OF MIND- to the mentally and physically challenged child and family in Israel. Shalva was founded on the premise that mentally and physically challenged children are not just the responsibility of the families to which they were born. "Heavens very special children," and their families, need and deserve the support of the extended community to be part of society and not apart.

Alyn Hospital (www.alyn.org), established almost 50 years ago, is one of the world's leading specialists in the active and intensive rehabilitation of children with a broad range of physical disabilities and is the only facility of its kind in Israel. Alyn is a non-profit organization treating children and adolescents with physical handicaps, regardless of religion or ethnic background.

Masorti (Conservative) Movement in Israel Special Needs programs (www.masorti.org/programs/specialneeds.html) Website includes information about bar/ bat mitzvah program, twinning programs, summer and post-high school programming.

Israel Guide Dog Center for the Blind (www.israelguidedog.org) The Israel Guide Dog Center for the Blind began operations on January 1, 1991 with just one objective -- to help blind people in Israel to achieve independence and mobility through the use of guide dogs. The mission of the Israel Guide Dog Center for the Blind is to improve the quality of life of blind people by providing them with safe mobility, independence and self-confidence through the faithful assistance of guide dogs.

The Lehiyot Program, (www.urj.org/jfc/lehiyot/) produced by the Department of Jewish Family Concerns, provides ideas and strategies on how to increase the inclusion of Jews with special needs in the congregational setting. Sponsored by the Union of Reform Judaism.

The National Jewish Council for the Disabled (http://www.ou.org/ncsy/njcd/nrc.htm) is dedicated to addressing the needs of all individuals with disabilities within the Jewish community. NJCD strives to enhance the life opportunities of people with special needs and to insure their participation in the full spectrum of Jewish life. Yachad provides unique social, educational and recreational "mainstreamed" programs for individuals (ages 8-40) with developmental disabilities. Our Way provides both mainstreamed and self-contained educational and recreational activities for the hearing-impaired and deaf.

RESOURCES FOR BUILDING ACCESSIBLE SYNAGOGUES

Adapted Living Spaces, 1160 Oakfield Drive, SE, Atlanta, GA 30316, 404-734-7343, www.adaptedlivingspaces.com

Presentations Gallery, LTD, 229 Washington Street, Mt. Vernon, NY 10553, 914-668-8181, www.PresentationsGallery.com, Bonnie Srolovitz, Michael Berkowicz, Assoc. AIA

Levin/Brown & Associates, Inc., 15 Greenspring Valley Road, Owings Mills, MD 21117, 1-800-296-9060, Jay Brown, AIA, Mark Levin, AIA

FlexPew Flexible Seating Systems, LLC, Reading Tables, PO Box 1035, Jenkintown, PA 19046-7335, 1-888-484-6565, www.FlexibleSeats.com, info@Flexible Seats.com

APPENDIX C -- HOSPITALITY ON A BUDGET
Inexpensive Ways to Become
A Welcoming Congregation[xl]

❑ Involve persons with disabilities in all planning for architectural modifications. Money is wasted when unusable modifications are made. Use the Americans with Disabilities Act (ADA) specifications to ensure success.

❑ Consider replacing fixed pews with flexible seating. This will turn your worship space into a multipurpose space, which will allow people with disabilities to participate fully in the life of your congregation.

❑ Cut the ends of several existing pews so that wheelchair users may be seated with their families rather than in specially designated, segregated sections.

❑ If there are steps to your sanctuary and/or Bimah, consider holding the service on the floor. This allows elderly persons and persons with disabilities to share in aliyahs in exactly the same way as the rest of the congregation.

❑ Think about converting two side-by-side bathrooms into one accessible unisex bathroom. Allow enough space for a wheelchair to turn around, and be sure to allow transfer space on both sides of the toilet. Use the ADA Accessibility Guidelines (ADAAG) and ask people with disabilities, who know what works and what doesn't, for important insight.

❑ Install long-handled door hardware, which is easier for everyone to use, especially those with impaired hand function.

❑ If wheelchair users volunteer in your office, consider raising the height of your work surfaces so that the wheelchairs can fit comfortably at a desk or table.

❑ Provide a paper cup dispenser near your water fountain. This will transform an inaccessible fountain into one accessible to wheelchair users. And remember, to keep the dispenser filled with cups!

❑ Suggest that congregants who are hard of hearing sit close to the front of the sanctuary where they can see the Rabbi and Cantor. Ask the Rabbi and Cantor to speak distinctly and slowly and to look frequently at the congregation since much lip reading takes place with persons who are hearing impaired. Seeing the facial expression of the speaker facilitates understanding of the spoken word both for people who read lips and those who don't. Always use the available sound system. When updating the sound system, be aware of new technologies, and consider installing an Assistive Listening System which we all have need of as we age.

❑ Survey your sound system to make sure it meets the needs of those with high-frequency sound loss. Install headphones in selected pews, if necessary. Familiarize the congregation with availability of all hearing devices.

❑ When remodeling or updating the existing Synagogue campus, install both a light and sound-cued fire alarm system. You may not have a person in the congregation who is deaf or severely hearing impaired now, but you may in the future.

❑ Check out resources and teaching aids that are available from public and private schools for children with special needs. They are usually easy to adapt for religious education programs.

❑ With local, state, and national organizations that focus on a specific problem, such as the Organization for the Visually Handicapped, Mental Illness Network, American Speech and Hearing Association, Council for Exceptional Children, CHADD, etc. ask specifically for names of people who might be able to help.

❑ Formally establish a "Committee" in your Synagogue to maintain regular communication with persons who are hospitalized, have recently returned home, or are dealing with difficult life situations. Very few people choose to be "homebound.' Being made to feel a continuing part of the religious community can often prevent losing vital people to depression and isolation

❑ Discover and utilize sources of large print, audio taped, or Braille books, magazines and *Tanakh*s. Audio taping materials for persons who are blind or have low vision is a wonderful outreach program for youth ministry. It is a service project that anyone who can read can do. No hammers required.

❑ Apply brightly colored, textured stripes at the tops of stairs to indicate that stairs are being approached. This will not only help persons with low vision, but also any person carrying something which blocks his/her vision.

❑ Make a survey of current lighting to ensure that the wattage is high enough and that the placement of fixtures ensures maximum visibility.

❑ If you have persons with severe visual impairments in your congregation, install signage in Braille or raised letters. When remodeling or updating the campus, install signage in Braille or raised letters. You may not have anyone in the congregation now who is blind or has a visual impairment, but you may in the future. It is a sign of hospitality.

❑ Make large print materials easy to casually pick up. Requesting "special" accommodations embarrasses many people, especially those of the "fifty-something" age group. Many Synagogues have simply raised the font size of print material to a minimum of 18 point.

❑ Make yourself knowledgeable of the needs and frustrations of those persons with invisible disabilities, such as chronic pain, diabetes, epilepsy, high blood pressure, mental illness, etc.

❑ Develop discussion about, and/or group support for, conditions such as diabetes, cancer, epilepsy, stroke, mental illness, etc. An adult education session or "second hour" presentation is an ideal time to share information about these disabilities. People with disabilities are excellent resources as are health care professionals.

❑ Check with USCJ's Committee on Accessibility for materials you may adapt and projects you can use related to disability access.

❑ In the context of a *Tanakh* study or perhaps in a sermon, explore the differences between "healing" and "cure." All people can receive God's healing grace; not all persons will be cured.

❑ Plan an adult education segment to discuss the non-architectural barriers to inclusiveness. A great educational opportunity!

❑ Hold all committee meeting and Synagogue-related activities in areas accessible to all.

❑ Use resources and show one or more of the excellent videotapes available about disability concerns. Many are available through the Interfaith Disabilities Network, secular press and faith-based media searches.

❑ Enlist the expertise of your congregants (carpenters, plumbers, contractors, persons with disabilities, teachers, social workers, nurses, etc.) to accomplish simple accessibility and awareness tasks. Always be guided by the specifications of the American with Disabilities Act (ADA).

❑ Develop a section of resources on disability concerns for the Synagogue library.

❑ Look for educational opportunities about disability and disability issues in your community.

❑ Encourage congregants to designate memorial gifts for accessibility projects.

❑ Visit accessible Synagogues in your area. Establish a mentoring relationship.

❑ Share your facilities with organizations that serve persons with disabilities and chronic illness.

❑ Set aside a bulletin board to display information and materials related to your accessibility project or issues of disability concerns.

❑ Explore ways of including members of your congregation with disabilities in the education, committee leadership, as well as in the worship of the congregation.

❑ Volunteer time at a day care center, hospital, or rehabilitation center so that you may come to know and understand persons with disabilities better.

❑ Be respectful of the food allergies and special diets of members. Strictly adhere to food prohibitions when preparing food. This can be a life-threatening situation! Be safe and label ingredients!

❑ Educate yourself and your congregants about environmental illness.

❑ Designate your Synagogue and meetinghouse a nonsmoking area.

❑ Suggest that your parishioners monitor the quantity of perfume, hair spray, or aftershave they use.

❑ Since many members of your congregation are employers and two-thirds of all people with severe disabilities are unemployed, become knowledgeable about issues around employment of persons who are disabled, both from the employers' and the employees' viewpoint.

❑ Develop a team of congregants willing to contact elected officials to lobby for legislation in the areas of accessible transportation and housing, employment for all who wish to work, community-based attendant care, and deinstitutionalization of people with disabilities. Support the American with Disabilities Act (ADA) of 1990—the Civil Rights act of people with disabilities!

❑ Celebrate Access Shabbat on a designated Saturday in October (national Disability and Employment month) or whenever convenient. Liturgy and other resource materials can be obtained through your denomination or the Interfaith Disabilities Network.

❑ Advertise your wheelchair access, hearing devices, large print materials, etc., when listing your services in the newspaper or other directory. This is a symbol of welcome and sign of acceptance to many people with disabilities who feel alienated from their Synagogue and ultimately from God. Use universal access symbols. You can obtain additional information from USCJ's Committee on Accessibility or from www.uscj.org/accessibility.

❑ Be of support and encouragement to parents of children with disabilities and to the children themselves. Children with disabilities can be integrated into religious education programs and the life of the Synagogue community. The presence of disability does not dissolve rights of passage, such as confirmation, Bar/Bat Mitzvah, etc. Resources and a bibliography can be obtained through the Interfaith Disabilities Network and USCJ's Committee on Accessibility.

APPENDIX D—ACADEMIC ACCOMODATIONS

Pointers for Talking to Faculty About Academic Accommodations[xli]

Going to college is a major transition whether you are coming straight from high school or returning to pursue your education after being away for a few years. Students with disabilities have all the concerns that students without disabilities have, plus issues related to having a disability. Successful students learn early in the transition process that they must take ownership of their disabilities.

Tips From Students

- Disclose your disability to Disability Support Services staff as early as possible, provide documentation of it, and let DSS staff help you to assess your needs and to plan each semester carefully.
- Learn to not be ashamed or embarrassed about having a disability. Understand that asking for assistance is not a sign of weakness or dependence.
- Use accommodations available for classroom, laboratories, and testing situations; for computer labs and library research; for tutorial and other academic enhancement services; for career counseling and planning needs; for student organization meetings and activities.
- Balance the time needed for non-academic, personal responsibilities and the time needed for learning course material-in college you are in class much less time than in high school, but are expected to spend many more hours on homework.
- Become skilled at negotiating the physical environment for maximum independence and access to all buildings, services, and programs.
- Continually improve your organizational skills and time management strategies.
- Make suggestions for physical and other access improvements at to the DSS office, and consider serving on the Chancellor's Committee on the ADA, a committee that decides how funds set aside for access issues will be spent each year.

1. Provide documentation of your disability to your campus' office and request a letter to share with your teachers.
2. Introduce yourself before or directly after the first class period and make an appointment to go to your professor's office where you can talk in private.
3. Be on time for your appointment. Be business-like, confident, pleasant, and respectful. Practice an assertive, reasonable approach to communicating your needs.
4. State your disability in simple terms. For example, I have muscular dystrophy; I am partially sighted; I am hard of hearing; or I have a learning disability. While you are not required to identify the specific disability, this information is often helpful to your professors.
5. Explain how your disability may affect you in completing the requirements of that course in the regular manner. Know what you can and cannot do and state it plainly.
6. "I cannot take my own notes because I have to watch your lips to understand what you're saying."
   - "My learning disability affects my reading and writing skills. Sometimes words look different to me than they actually are. I have trouble with spelling and often get letters and words turned around or mixed up. It

takes me longer to read and write but I do usually understand the information I'm dealing with."

7. Suggest a method of accommodation that will work for you. Tell the professor what you need.

    - "I need to get a copy of another student's notes. I can send around a notice to find someone if that's okay. I would prefer not to be pointed out directly in class, but rather have volunteers come forward after class to meet me, or leave their names and phone *Bamidbar* with you. If you know a good student in the class you might ask that person directly."

    - "I'm using books on tape because my learning disability affects my processing of printed words and letters. I'll also need to take my exams orally-they can be recorded on tape so you won't need to actually read them to me while I take the test."

8. Be willing to listen if the professor makes alternative suggestions. Be reasonable. Take into consideration individual preferences of teachers and be willing to try reasonable alternatives if they will work for you. There often is more than one way to accomplish the same goal.

9. Do not hesitate to speak up, however, if the suggested alternative method is not satisfactory for your needs. Just be prepared to explain why it doesn't work for you.

10. Communicate to the professor that you are interested in meeting all requirements and standards of the course just like everyone else, but that you need to do things in a way that is different from the usual manner because of your disability.

APPENDIX E – A FEW ALPHABETS

American Sign Language (ASL)	Hebrew Manual Alphabet
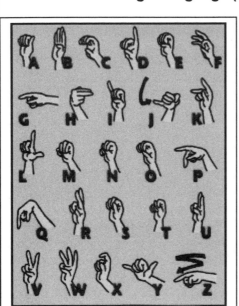	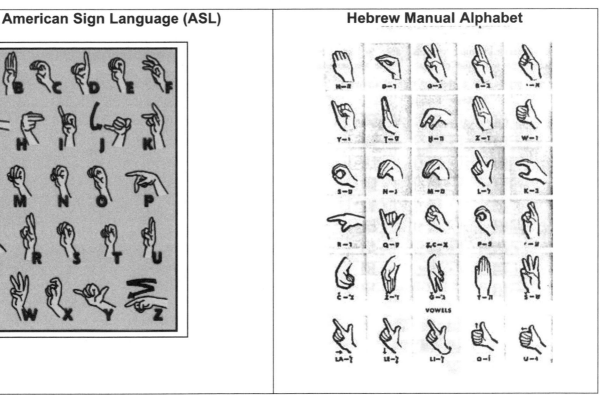

Hebrew Braille

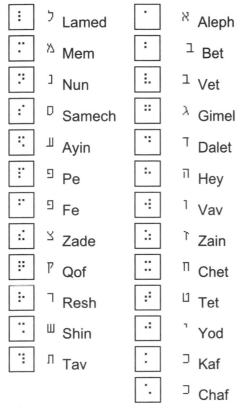

ל Lamed	א Aleph		
א Mem	בּ Bet		
נ Nun	ב Vet		
ס Samech	ג Gimel		
ע Ayin	ד Dalet		
פּ Pe	ה Hey		
פ Fe	ו Vav		
צ Zade	ז Zain		
ק Qof	ח Chet		
ר Resh	ט Tet		
ש Shin	י Yod		
ת Tav	כּ Kaf		
	כ Chaf		

APPENDIX F--ATTITUDE QUESTIONS

EXERCISE

The following questions should be considered before you begin reading of this volume. After you have completed your study of the topic, consider them once again. Answer as honestly and frankly as possible.

1. Do you feel that Judaism has generally had a liberal, open-minded view toward those with disabilities?

2. Are there any ritual actions from which a person with a disability should be excluded?

3. What does the following biblical phrase mean to you: Do not put a stumbling block in front of the blind; do not curse the deaf?

4. Can a disability ever be a blessing? If so, how?

5. Did you ever have friend who has a disability? If so, did you ever ask him or her how it feels to have a disability? If you didn't have a friend who has a disability, were there any particular reasons?

6. Do you feel that Jewish institutions are generally accessible to people with disabilities? What about your synagogue?

7. Do you think that people who have a mental impairment should get married or have children?

8. Should someone who is deaf have a Bar/Bat mitzvah? What about someone who is blind? What about someone who has a mental impairment?

9. Why do you think some people are born with disabilities and others are not? Does this raise any questions for you about God?

10. Are there any recent developments which might, in your opinion, change Jewish views toward people with disabilities?

APPENDIX G -- DISABILITY ACCESS SYMBOLS

The twelve symbols below may be used to promote and publicize accessibility of places, programs and other activities for people with various disabilities. Any language accompanying the symbols should focus on the accommodation or service, not on who uses it. For example, "Ramped Entrance" may accompany the wheelchair symbol. This is important because not only do individuals in wheelchairs use ramps, but so do people with baby carriages, luggage, packages, etc. Language that fosters dignity is important too. For example, "Reserved Parking" or "Accessible Parking" may be used with the wheelchair symbol to indicate that parking spaces designated for people with disabilities.

Audio Description for TV, Video and Film

This service makes television, video, and film more accessible for persons who are blind or have low vision. Description of visual elements is provided by a trained Audio Describer through the Secondary Audio Program (SAP) of televisions and monitors equipped with stereo sound. An adapter for non-stereo TVs is available through the American Foundation for the Blind, (800)829-0500.

Accessibility Symbol

The wheelchair symbol should only be used to indicate access for individuals with limited mobility, including wheelchair users. For example, the symbol is used to indicate an accessible entrance, bathroom or that a phone is lowered for wheelchair users. Remember that a ramped entrance is not completely accessible if there are no curb cuts, and an elevator is not accessible if it can only be reached via steps.

Access to Low Vision

This symbol may be used to indicate access for people who are blind or have low vision, including: a guided tour, a path to a nature trail or a scent garden in a park; and a tactile tour or a museum exhibition that may be touched.

Telephone Typewriter (TTY)

Also known as text telephone (TT), or telecommunications device for the deaf (TDD), TTY indicates a telephone device used with the telephone (and the phone number) for communication between deaf, hard of hearing, speech-impaired and/or hearing persons.

Volume Control Telephone

This symbol indicates the location of telephones that have handsets with amplified sound and/or adjustable volume controls.

Sign Language Interpretation

The symbol indicates that Sign Language Interpretation is provided for a lecture, tour, performance, conference or other program.

Braille Symbol

This symbol indicates that printed matter is available in Braille.

Braille

Assistive Listening Systems

These systems transmit sound via hearing aids or head sets. They include infrared, loop and FM systems. Portable systems may be available from the same audiovisual equipment suppliers that service conferences and meetings.

Accessible Print

The symbol for large print is 'Large Print' printed in 18 Point or larger text. In addition to indicating that large print versions of books, pamphlets, museum guides and theater

programs are available, you may use the symbol on conference or membership forms to indicate that print materials may be provided in large print. Sans serif or modified serif print with good contrast is highly recommended, and special attention should be paid to letter and word spacing.

The Information Symbol

The most valuable commodity of today's society is information; to a person with a disability it is essential. For example, the symbol may be used on signage or on a floor plan to indicate the

location of the information or security desk, where there is more specific information or materials concerning access accommodations and services such as "LARGE PRINT" materials, audio cassette recordings of materials, or sign interpreted tours.

Closed Captioning (CC)

This symbol indicates that a television program or videotape is closed captioned for deaf or hard of hearing persons (and others). TV sets that have a built-in or a separate decoder are equipped to display dialogue for programs that are captioned. The Television Decoder Circuitry Act of 1990 requires new TV sets (with screens 13" or larger) to have built-in decoders as of July, 1993. Also, videos that are part of exhibitions may be closed captioned using the symbol with instructions to press a button for captioning. The alternative would be open captioning, which translates dialogue and other sounds in print.

Live Audio Description

A service for people who are blind or have low vision that makes the performing and visual arts more accessible. A trained Audio Describer offers live commentary or narration (via headphones and a small

transmitter) consisting of concise, objective descriptions of visual elements: for example, a theater performance or a visual arts exhibition at a museum.

The Disability Access Symbols were produced by the Graphic Artists Guild Foundation with support and technical assistance from the Office for Special Constituencies, National Endowment for the Arts. Special thanks to the National Endowment for the Arts. Graphic design assistance by the Society of Environmental Graphic Design. Consultant: Jacqueline Ann Clipsham.
www.gag.org/resources/das.html

APPENDIX H -- Usable Type
Prepared by USCJ's Committee on Accessibility
March 2003[xlii]

Many programs and events rely heavily on printed information, both as part of the advertising campaign and during the event itself. The design of type and how it is applied should be considered, among other avenues, for **newspaper ads**, **board minutes**, **budget information**, **fliers**, **event programs**, **name badges**, **schedules**, **maps**, and **exhibit descriptions**.

The following are some general parameters that will help you design printed pieces to make them more usable to the general population as well as people with vision disabilities.

People with limited vision need printed material that is...
- Easy to read, especially if the information is to be read quickly, and in less than ideal circumstances, such as while walking, at night, or at distance.
- Type should be simple and contrast highly with the background.
- When graphics are included, they should be clear and not overprinted onto type.

To make printed materials legible for the largest percentage of the population, they should be prepared...

With content that
- Uses clear, on-technical English in the active voice.
- Has limited sentence length of fewer than 25 words. If possible, keep each sentence to one thought only.
- When in the form of instructional text, it is formatted in either a bulleted or numbered list, usually limited to three or four items per list.

With type design that
- Uses sans-serif or simple serif type faces. Limit the number of typeface varieties to two or three. Examples of sans serif typefaces include Helvetica, Univers, Arial, and Futura. Suggested simple serif typefaces include New Century Schoolbook and Palatino.
- Uses bold face type for single-page fliers that are posted, for example on a bulletin board.
- Is presented in 16-point type size when possible so most participants read it easily.

Examples of Sans-serif Typefaces	Examples of Simple Serif Typefaces	Do Not Use the Following Type Styles
Arial Helvetica **Verdana**	**New Century Schoolbook** Palatino	*Script type* **Condensed type** **Extended type** Light type *Ornate italic type*

- Use line spaces of one and one-half spaces or is double spaced
- Uses lower case letters with initial capitals.
- Avoids underlining except in headings
- Justifies text on left side only. Type that is justified both left and right hinders legibility because it introduces awkward spaces between words that people do not recognize, making text more difficult to read.
- Where narrow columns of text are used, provides at least an inch of white space between columns.

With type and background that
- Contrast with each other. (Characters contrast with background by at least 70%). Avoid combinations such as yellow on gray.
- Are opaque with the use of non-glossy colors and materials. A medium with a matte or other non-glare finish should be used for both the background and the text.

You should strive to produce all printed materials in at least 16 or 18-point type to be readable both by people with low vision and by sighted people. This can be accomplished by using a photocopier to enlarge existing type if this provides good ink coverage or by using a computer / word processor. Even the most rudimentary computers often have the capability of generating type in different fonts, sizes and weights.

The symbol for large print is 'Large Print' In addition to indicating that large print **guides** and **programs** are available, you **conference** or **membership forms** to be provided in large print. Sans serif or contrast is highly recommended, and to letter and word spacing.

printed in **18 Point** or larger text. versions of **books**, **pamphlets**, may use the symbol on indicate that print materials may modified serif print with good special attention should be paid

16-point type
16-point bold type
ALL CAPS ARE HARD TO READ IN CONTINUOUS TEXT
Use of Initial Caps in Headlines is Preferred

Appendix I—Organizations Supported by USY's TIKUN OLAM Fund

AKIM

Akim is a voluntary association in Jerusalem and surrounding areas that provides assistance to mentally retarded and developmentally disabled adults whose old and ailing parents can no longer care for them at home. Akim provides educational, residential, and leisure time services for about 1000 persons, while always researching for new and creative models of service delivery.
Website: www.akim-jerusalem.org.il

ALYN

The Alyn Woldenberg Orthopedic Hospital and Rehabilitation Center for physically handicapped children in Israel treats patients up to 18 years of age, offering physiotherapy, occupational therapy and treatment to disabled children. Alyn services 100 in-patients, 20 day patients and has a lengthy waiting list. In the past, our funds have been used for special trips, the outpatient clinic, music therapy programs, and new orthopedic appliances.
Website: www.alyn.org

CENTER FOR THE ADVANCEMENT OF THE BLIND

The Center provides year round programs for blind individuals of all backgrounds and ages. Their clients include both those who have been blind for their entire lifetime as well as those who have recently become blind. They have residential rehabilitation programs, summer camps, pre-schools, computer workshops for the visually impaired, and daytime programs in and around Safed.
Website: www.beityael.org

DYSAUTONOMIA FOUNDATION

The foundation promotes research into a rare hereditary disease that afflicts only Ashkenazic Jews. The disease is a malfunction of the autonomic nervous system, which controls involuntary processes, such as swallowing, sucking, the opening of the tear ducts, and the awareness of the sensations of hot and cold. Money is needed to promote extensive research to prevent dysautonomia in unborn children. Twenty-five percent of all dysautonomic children die by the age of ten because of complications.
Website: www.familialdysautonomia.org

EMTZA REGION SPECIAL NEEDS PROGRAM

Emtza Region USY's "L'taken Olam: Bridging the Gap" Special Needs Fund enables USYers with special needs to attend regional USY events. Emtza Region USY has partnered with the Tikvah Program of Camp Ramah in Wisconsin to identify and recruit potential USYers, and these funds go towards the cost of training and bringing specialized staff to the regional USY events.
Website: www.emtza.org

GAN TAZPIT

A diagnostic Kindergarten for the developmentally disabled, there are currently 40 children between the ages of three and seven at Gan Tazpit. They are grouped in five classes and their progress is encouraged and recorded by a director, two speech therapists, five teachers, an occupational therapist, a play therapist, etc. These are all children with delayed development. As recently as ten years ago, they would have been classified as retarded, and thus doomed to a lifetime of institutional environment, but now they are treated from an early age in the hope that they can go on to lead normal lives.

HAIFA CENTER FOR CHILDREN WITH LEARNING DISABILITIES

The Haifa Center for Children with Learning Disabilities is a school for learning disabled students. The Center provides enrichment programs for children who are still enrolled in their regular schools. They also do outreach within the community to try and overcome the stereotypes of the learning disabled. This year our funds are going towards equipment for their special ed kindergarten.
E-mail: ladder@netvision.net.il

HAMA IL

Hama Il, Humans and Animals in Mutual Assistance in Israel, is dedicated to Animal Assisted Therapy, Education, and Activities, but with a difference – the animals they use are primarily abused animals that have been rescued and saved from death. This in and of itself has a tremendous impact on the people they work with, which includes rape victims, domestic violence victims, autistic children, Holocaust survivors, etc. Hama Il is actively involved in rehabilitation programs in Israeli hospitals, schools, prisons, crisis intervention and family guidance clinics and day care centers. USY Pilgrimage groups have recently had the opportunity to witness the miracles that occur at Hama Il on a daily basis. E-mail: hama-israel@bezeqint.net

HEVRAH PROGRAM

The Hevrah Program was founded in 1995 by the Far West Region of USY in conjunction with Camp Ramah in California. Based on the Tikvah "Buddy Program" at Camp Ramah, the Hevrah Program brings together Jewish teens with special needs and active USYers. While the Tikvah Buddy Program takes place during the summer at camp, the Hevrah Program is available year-round in an urban setting. The program also provides educational programs for the USYers about the special needs associated with having a disability. Website: www.fwusy.net

ILAN (JERUSALEM)

The Israel Foundation for Handicapped Children takes care of over 10,000 persons afflicted with neuromuscular handicaps, including individuals with polio, etc. As the largest voluntary organization in Israel, ILAN gives medical, educational, vocational, welfare and social attention and treatment to patients. The Sabin Scholarship Fund provides fees and maintenance for 1950 Polio Epidemic victims. Our funds help to provide special programming for the people at one of the sheltered workshops in Jerusalem, as well as equipment for their new workshop.
E-mail: ilanjr@netvision.net.il

ILAN (HAIFA)

Also affiliated with the National Ilan framework (described above), our funds to this branch of Ilan are being used to construct and equip a sports and rehabilitation center for handicapped children in Haifa and the Northern part of Israel. E-mail: ilanhai@netvision.net.il

ISRAEL ELWYN

Israel Elwyn provides rehabilitation and training services to children and adults with disabilities, including persons with developmental disabilities, Cerebral Palsy, autism, and physical and sensory impairments. Programs include vocational rehabilitation and training, supported employment, community-based group homes, special education schools, preschool programs, medical and dental services and adult development centers. Israel Elwyn currently serves more than 780 individuals in four major locations, in both East and West Jerusalem. Web Site: www.israelelwyn.org.il

ISRAEL GUIDE DOG CENTER FOR THE BLIND
Founded in 1991 the Israel Guide Dog Center's mission is to help blind people in Israel achieve independence and mobility. Prior to the opening of the Center, blind Israelis had to travel to the United States to get guide dogs. Aside from being prohibitively expensive for most Israelis the situation also posed a language barrier challenge both for the clients as well as the dogs that had been trained in English. The Center breeds and trains dogs as well as provides follow-up care for all of its clients to make sure the partnership is working. Website: www.israelguidedog.org

ISRAEL NATIONAL THERAPEUTIC RIDING ASSOCIATION
The former Therapeutic Riding Club was established in 1986. Its purpose is to promote the recovery of disabled individuals through horseback riding, support related medical research and to train and certify therapeutic riding instructors. Therapeutic riding helps improve muscle tone, balance, posture, coordination, motor development and emotional and physical well-being. USY Pilgrimage groups often have the chance to witness the incredible miracles that occur at INTRA daily. Website: www.intra.org.il

JEWISH BRAILLE INSTITUTE OF AMERICA
Centered in New York, the Jewish Braille Institute provides services for the Jewish Blind throughout North America. This includes religious training through tapes and transcription of Braille materials in Hebrew such as Siddurim and Chumashim. Our contributions have been used for the low vision center in Tel-Aviv, to expand the tape library in New York, to print a large-print edition of the Torah, and for programs in Eastern Europe. Website: www.jbilibrary.org

KEREN OR CENTER
This is the only Jewish residential institution in the world devoted exclusively to the care and rehabilitation of blind children and youth with multiple disabilities, many of whom have been abandoned by their parents because of their complicated needs. Our funds are being used to help purchase physiotherapy equipment as well as playground equipment for the Center.
Website: www.keren-or.org

KESHER
Established to fill the gap in the health care system for families with children with disabilities and chronic illnesses in Israel. Kesher provides information assistance, counseling and referrals, and is the only service designed specifically to help parents and families to cope better with everyday difficulties of raising their children. Website: www.mrkesher.org.il

MICHA (JERUSALEM)
Micha's programs work to enable the deaf child from early age to use his residual hearing and activate his sense of understanding and speech development and help him enjoy his childhood like other children. Our funds have helped to purchase books, toys, playground equipment, and hearing aids for the children.
E-mail:micha_jr@netvision.net.il

MISHOLIM

The Jerusalem Expressive Therapy Center for Children is run by a group of educators and therapists who have specialized in the treatment of children with emotional and organic problems. Such children have difficulty expressing themselves and establishing the interpersonal relationships necessary for their normal development. Therefore, they need a special program in which use is made of creative and expressive methods as the means of treatment--plastic, arts, movement, drama and music. Website: www.misholim.org.il

NATIONAL TAY SACHS FOUNDATION

This non-profit, philanthropic organization was formed to raise funds for, and to promote research into Tay-Sachs and allied neurodegenerative diseases of infancy and childhood; to support and promote programs of carrier detection and prevention; and to assist the families of afflicted children by making available to them counseling facilities, out-patient clinics and the opportunity to participate in the purposes and programs of the association.
Website: www.ntsad.org

NEVE MENASHE

The Neve Menashe Home is the largest home for the mentally handicapped in Israel. There are over 400 residents aged 14-70. Most of the residents are severely retarded and about 80 of them are also physically handicapped, which requires a staff of nearly 300. They live in groups of 24 persons to a house. The home is now gradually being rebuilt by government funds, as it is very old. Unfortunately the government does not provide more than the bare essentials.
Website: www.nevemenashe.com

REENA FOUNDATION

The Canada-based Reena Foundation's ultimate goal is to maximize the potential of Jewish men and women who are developmentally handicapped in an effort to support them towards independent living within their communities. The program includes residential services, support groups, travel programs (including to Israel), and recreational activities.
Website: www.reena.org

SHAI SOCIETY – BEIT HAGALGALIM

Shai Society, also known as Beit Hagalgalim (house on wheels), provides moral support and rehabilitation activities for physically handicapped people between ages 10 and 30. They invite these people to spend weekends at Beit Hagalgalim, where they learn how to integrate into society and acquire independence. All their staff are made up of volunteers, some of who graduated the program themselves. Website: www.hasamabg.co.il

SHALVA

Shalva was officially opened in June 1990 in Israel. Shalva provides services for children with mental and physical disabilities, all of which are offered free of charge. Shalva works under the premise that children will thrive and develop more in a home situation than if they are institutionalized. Shalva provides support and assistance to parents so that they can cope with the challenges and pressures of bringing up a child with disabilities.
Website: www.shalva.org

SHEKEL/PROGRAMS FOR SPECIAL NEEDS CHILDREN
This program creates educational and recreational programs for special needs children and children from dysfunctional homes in Jerusalem. Our funds are used to help provide materials for their parent and child center, as well as towards their "Adopt a child for Shabbat" program.
Website: www.shekel.org.il

TIKVAH PROGRAMS OF CAMP RAMAH
The Tikvah Program is an exciting experiment in Jewish Education that offers a chance for "special" teens with learning difficulties to join the Jewish community of Camp Ramah for the summer. There, in an integrated setting, the campers participate in classes, swimming, sports, and all other activities available to the Ramah camper. Where the Tikvah campers have special needs, they receive special education; where they have strengths, they are given every opportunity to build on them. Tikvah programs exist at Ramah camps in New England, Wisconsin, Canada, and California.
Website: www.campramah.org/tikvah.html

TSAD KADIMA
Tsad Kadima (A Step Forward) is an association of professionals and parents of children with cerebral palsy. The association was responsible for bringing the Hungarian Peto method of Conductive Education to Israel. This educational rehabilitation system's aim is to teach children with cerebral palsy to overcome their motor disabilities and to be functionally independent. Tsad Kadima operates several kindergarten and elementary classes in both Jerusalem and greater Tel Aviv. They also have supplementary education programs for adolescents as well as a camping program. Website: www.tsadkadima.co.il

ABOUT THE AUTHOR

CARL ASTOR is currently Rabbi of Congregation Beth El in New London, Connecticut, where accessibility for people with disabilities has been an issue for several years. He previously served in the pulpit of the Wayne Conservative Congregation in Wayne, New Jersey.

In 1974, Rabbi Astor was ordained by The Jewish Theological Seminary of America, where he also received his M.A. In addition, he has completed all course work toward a doctoral degree in Midrash from the Seminary. He received his B.A. from the University of Pennsylvania, having spent one year at the Hebrew University of Jerusalem during his undergraduate studies.

Rabbi Astor has been involved with numerous educational programs of the Conservative Movement. He has held many roles at Camp Ramah, including counselor, Division Head, and Director of Tzibbur, a work/study program. In addition, he has completed marathon races, including the New York City Marathon, for several years.

He and his wife, Sharon, have three children, Sara, Avi, and Donniel

ENDNOTES

i   Orah Hayyim, Hilchot B'rachot, 22.5.9.

ii   Helen Keller, *The Story of My Life* (Garden City, NY Doubleday & Company 1954) 16.

iii   Excerpted from Americans with Disabilities Association website: http://www.adata.org/whatsada-definition.html, © 2004.

iv   This division is based on *Encyclopedia Britannica*, 15th ed., s.v. "*Education of the Exceptional*," by Samuel A Kirk.

v   Some information in this section was reprinted with permission from the University of Arkansas.

vi   Excerpted from *Mishneh Ha-Briyyot: A New Jewish Approach to Disabilities* by Rabbi Elliot N. Dorff, Ph.D., HUC-JIR Kalsman Institute on Judaism and Health, May 2003.

vii Commandment 275. This and the previous citation of Maimonides are found in Edward Kaminetzky, *Sins of Omission: The Neglected Children* (New York: Yeshiva University Press, Department of Special Publications, 1977), 92.

viii Excerpted from "*Blemished People, Unblemished Tools*," by Rabbi Bradley Shavit Artson, 2001

ix   Excerpted from "*A Miracle Kadimanik*", *Kol Kadima*, Winter 1995, United Synagogue Youth

x   See *Encyclopedia Judaica*, s.v. :hazakah," by M. Elon.

xi   Mishneh Torah, Hilchot To'en 13:2.

xii   Mishneh Torah, Hilchot Mehirah 29:3-4.

xiii The interpretation was cited in Chapter 3.

xiv Herbert Schwartz, "*To Open the Ears of the Deaf*," *Conservative Judaism*, vol. 28 no. 2 (Winter, 1974), 62.

xv   The author is grateful to Judith May, Clinical Supervisor of the Department of Audiology at the New York League for the Hard of Hearing, for clarifying this material.

xvi Schwartz, "To Open the Ears," 63.

xvii Fortner, "Caring for people with disabilities."

xviii Publications of the London Beit Din, no. 10, 1963 (in Hebrew).

xix Used with Permission from Becca Hornstein, Council for Jews with Special Needs, Phoenix, AZ

xx   Based on Louis Ginzberg, *The Legends of the Jews* (Philadelphia: The Jewish Publication Society of America, 1909-38), vol. 1, 328-29.

xxi Based on Ginzberg, *The Legends of the Jews*, vol. 2, 324-25.

xxii Based on Ginzberg, *The Legends of the Jews*, vol. 2, 359.

xxiii Based on Ginzberg, *The Legends of the Jews*, vol. 1, 421-22.

xxiv Tanhuma Buber: Vayigash 104b.

xxv Literally, "of enlightened eyes"; the phrase is discussed below.

xxvi Reprinted from Danny Siegel: Why Blind People Should have Cars. Solved by: John Fling, Mitzvah hero, Columbia, SC, who tries to make sure his many blind friends have microwave ovens.

xxvii Personal conversations, newspaper articles, television coverage. In February, 1994, the author was with Mr. Fling once again, and he was reminded of a child, about 11 or 12, who was dying of a brain tumor. She had said she really wanted a TV. (She was already blind.) When Mr. Sig Friedman, one of Mr. Fling's friends, offered to donate one, it was a black and white set, but she said she would prefer a color TV. Her reason was that the sound was better on the color set, but Mr. Friedman and Mr. Fling both understood it was really for her parents. It was both eye-opening and heartbreaking to hear the story told to me. Many similar tales come from the Make a Wish Foundation.

xxviii Harold Kushner, *When Bad Things Happen to Good People* (New York: Schocken Books, Inc., 1981), 29-30.

xxix (Used with permission from Rabbi Bradley Shavit Artson. Rabbi Artson is the Dean of the Ziegler School of Rabbinic Studies, Bel Air, California, and the author of Dear Rabbi: Jewish Answers to Life's Questions, forthcoming from Alef Publishing.)